The Ghosts of Dartmouth

by

Christine Donnelly

© Christine Donnelly 2019

The right of Christine Donnelly to be identified as the author of this work has been asserted by her in accordance with the Copyright, Designs and Patents Act 1988.

Edited by Ken Taylor
Layout & design by Archyve
For picture credits see page 103

The design and contents are copyright and may not be reproduced apart from fair use (e.g. for private research), in any form without written permission from the publisher.

First published in the United Kingdom in 2019 by

Dark Faery Books

darkfaerybooks@gmail.com
Printed in the United Kingdom
ISBN 978-1-9160918-0-1
3 5 7 9 10 8 6 4 2

Disclaimer

These stories are offered in good faith: the author has researched them as thoroughly as practical, and to the best of her knowledge they are true in the sense that each witness has described an actual experience. The interpretation of such experiences is speculative, and no claim for the empirical existence of ghosts or other phenomena included in this book is given or should be inferred.

If you think you may have a problem with any aspect of the paranormal, seek suitably qualified help. But remember, supernatural events are rare so don't give yourself nightmares.

Contents

Thanks & Acknowledgements	4
Preface, by Ken Taylor	5
The Phantom Ship of Warfleet Bay, Dartmouth	6
Introduction	7
Dartmouth Museum	8
Haunting at the Start Bay Inn, Torcross	11
Market Street, Dartmouth	21
Disturbances at Dartmouth	24
The Spinning Wheel Café, Dartmouth	26
Nethway House, Kingswear	28
Poltergeist Activity, Dartmouth	35
The Church of St Petrox, Dartmouth	37
Haunting at Slapton Sands	40
Ghostly Encounter with a Cream Cake, Dartmouth	48
Mount Boone, Dartmouth	49
Dartmouth Castle	50
Guardians from the Past, Strete Gate	58
Coastguard Cottages, Dartmouth	59
Ghostly Activity in Archway Drive, Dartmouth	61
The Old Ambulance HQ, Dartmouth	62
A Chilling Experience at Alma Place, Kingswear	65
Disturbance at The Royal Castle Hotel, Dartmouth	67
The Mantle of Cornu, a Blackawton Tale	69
Tragedy at the Britannia Royal Naval College, Dartmouth	71
Eight Short Stories	72
The George Inn	76
An initial investigation	78
The second investigation	81
Psychometry	83
Meanwhile back at the Inn...	85
Psychic art	85
Dowsing	88
Automatic writing	93
Shadows of the past	96
Tracey's diary	98
A few final tales	99
Conclusion	101
Bibliography	102
Picture Credits	103
Index	103

Thanks & Acknowledgements

I owe a big thank-you to Ken Taylor for giving me the opportunity to write this sequel to *Dartmouth Ghosts and Mysteries*. I have been greatly inspired by Ken's work, who is the editor of this edition and the author of many other excellent books in his own right and of the first book of *Dartmouth Ghosts and Mysteries*, which was a huge success. He has also kindly written an account of his visit to Dartmouth Castle as a participant in a paranormal investigation. Ken and I have been friends for many years and I thank him for his patience and knowledge, and helping me along on the journey on which writing this book has taken me.

I also thank my partner Brian, who has had to listen to all my stories, whether he wanted to or not, and contend with my grumpy days when things just weren't going right. His support has been amazing and without him this book would not have been written.

I would like to say thank-you to Lorna Stimpson, a good friend, who has been very patient and provided much appreciated help with the book.

I would also like to thank everyone who has helped in making this book as good as it is, not only those mentioned in the text, but all those who made a significant contribution behind the scenes – especially Brian Reid, Dale Rossiter, Dartmouth Museum, Cookworthy Museum (Kingsbridge), and Dennis and Betty Hemmings.

Preface
by
Ken Taylor

There are themes in life which recur, spontaneously, and although each episode may seem complete, time shows us - again and again - that every conclusion is really just the passing of a milestone.

My journey with the paranormal in Dartmouth began in 1980 with an invitation to share an old fishing boat moored in Old Mill Creek. The offer came straight out of the blue, but I moved in as a lark, and stayed in Dartmouth for over five years. Just before I left, I self-published a collection of the supernatural stories I'd picked up along the way (I saw the book as a museum for spoken tales).

Twenty years later, while spring-cleaning, I came across my old folder of notes and I figured it was either time to discard them or... Well, a complex series of chance events culminated in *Dartmouth Ghosts & Mysteries*, published by Richard Webb in 2006.

Ten years after that, I wondered how the stories were developing, but I hadn't enough spare time even to begin researching the current situation. Fortunately I knew somebody who would enjoy such a project, and she wrote this book.

Will I continue to be haunted by Dartmouth? I'll certainly bear many memories - good, bad, fond, and sad - with me to the grave. The South Hams is a special place, full of remarkable people (especially, those who feel they're nothing out of the ordinary), and the spirit of the place only reveals her secrets at her own pace.

Usually, when I try to hurry Fate along I wind up chasing my own tail like some headless ghost stumbling around in circles, oblivious to what's right in front of me. Even so, now and again, I trip over something that turns out to be a milestone, and after I've dusted off the bruises, I see things more clearly again.

The paranormal is deeply mysterious and can be terrifying, so anything that shines a light on it is very welcome. We instinctively fear the unknown, yet despite the risks of an unfathomable abyss, we give our curiosity freedom to explore life, love, and our role in the cosmos. I applaud the author's courage and determination in writing this book, and to these pages, I welcome you.

The Phantom Ship of Warfleet Bay, Dartmouth

THE PHANTOM SHIP OF WARFLEET BAY.

'Twas the very witching hour of night,
  When graves give up their dead,
And Churchyards yawn and Ghosts come forth
  This Earth, once more, to tread.
I stood upon the Viaduct
  That faces Warfleet Bay,
I saw a weird a ghostly sight
  That haunts me night and day:
Within the Bay where now lies sunk
  The Spanish man-of-war,
A Phantom Ship appeared in sight
  Full rigged from aft to fore,
Her men were gathered on the deck,
  The Captain where was he?
Upon the main-yard arm he hung
  As dead as dead could be.
Full three times passed that Phantom Ship
  Before my startled eyes,
A blue flame seemed to light that corpse
  That hung 'twixt seas and skies.
Unearthly fire enwrapped the ship,
  A ghostly fearsome light,
Then 'neath the circumambient wave
  She vanished from my sight.

                    St. GEORGE.

Famously, poetry bridges the realms of fact and fiction (St George 1872).

Introduction

Dartmouth is a town steeped in history and mystery. Within its shadowy lanes and streets there lies a wealth of ghostly tales, both from its historical past and right up to present day. The people of Dartmouth go about their everyday lives but some find they are touched by strange events that they cannot make sense of. These are the people that have offered to tell of their weird and interesting encounters in this book.

I have conducted many talks on the subject of the paranormal and parapsychology and the one question that is most commonly asked is 'What are ghosts and why do some appear to be grounded and remain here?'

That is a question to which no one really knows the answer. Why when some people pass-over they are never seen again, but others are 'seen' and even appear to try to communicate with us. There are many theories why this happens, some of which are explored in this book, but they are still only theories. As time goes on, no doubt, even more theories will be put forward. Some theories are based on a spiritual point of view whilst others deal with it in a scientific way. Generally, it is thought that spirits remain here because they have 'unfinished business' and wish to conclude this before they move on.

The real question is 'What is it that we call Spirit?' Are spirits just echoes from the past, or are they from different dimensions? When we die, where do we go? Do we exist no more or do we simply pass into another dimension? Many people have seen orbs of light which are thought to be ghostly spirits, some people see a full body manifestation of a person. Both are entirely different aspects of the same thing, but why? Perhaps it depends on how our brains interpret the information that is given to us.

Whatever the answer is, the paranormal is truly a very interesting subject and I hope that you will continue to question it and look at it from both sides of the fence. There appears to be no definitive answer at this present day but perhaps in time, we will achieve a greater understanding of the subject.

Fireplace in the King's Room, Dartmouth Museum.

Dartmouth Museum

In Duke Street, Dartmouth, the terrace of rich merchants' houses, known as The Butterwalk, was built around 1640 - granite piers support the beautifully carved wooden facia. At the end of The Butterwalk stands Dartmouth Museum, a Grade 1 listed building.

Jan Murphy (*Mysteries and the Paranormal*) recently visited Dartmouth Museum and heard some strange stories related by the staff. They said that it is haunted by a mysterious cavalier who likes to stand by the fireplace in the King's Room. He has been seen many times over the years and his ghostly footsteps have also been heard, pacing up and down from time to time. He is known by some of the staff as 'Himself' which would seem to add some importance to the ghostly figure, as though he may have been a person of high standing.

King Charles II was sailing across the channel from Plymouth to London in July 1671 when a strong easterly wind threatened and he ordered that they should seek shelter in Dartmouth. What is now known as The King's Room was thought to be the best room in the town to receive the King.

He held court there for several hours and is said then to have continued on to Nethway House, Kingswear where he spent the night before proceeding to Exeter. The King's Room has beautiful wood panelling and an ornate ceiling, and the Royal Coat of Arms was placed above the fireplace in his honour. It is standing by this very fireplace that the ghostly figure has been seen.

There is no documentation that I can find that it has communicated with anyone, which would suggest that is perhaps a replay apparition. We can see it but it can't see us, it is unaware of us. It is similar to watching a loop recording, being periodically shown over and over again. It is an energy, which for various reasons has become imprinted on a place and is unable to communicate with us because it existed in another time.

Its ghostly footsteps have been heard occasionally pacing up and down, and other strange things have also been reported. Display items mysteriously move around by themselves, in particular tiny figures in the doll's house, which are encased in a glass cabinet.

The interior of the doll's house was created by Ursula Dimes, a descendant of the last family to live at Oldstone Mansion, Blackawton. She recreated rooms using designs taken from diaries, drawings, stories and photos handed down to her from her family. I have seen the doll's house and it is locked away in a heavy glass cabinet. The door to the cabinet can be difficult to open and it is always kept locked with a key. How or why these tiny figures are moved about is a mystery.

There is yet another strange thing that has been noted from time to time and that is the smell of tobacco smoke. The museum is a smoke free zone. Of course it may be that smoke is drifting up the stairs from the outside. To get into the museum you go through an outer door into a small hallway and then up a flight of stairs which then turn halfway up onto the first floor of the building. If the smoke was coming from outside the building you would imagine that it would dissipate considerably on its journey up into the building, making its origin something of a mystery.

The Oldstone Mansion doll's house, Dartmouth Museum.

Haunting at the Start Bay Inn, Torcross

The village of Torcross lies on the coast at the southern end of Slapton Sands. Violent storms and the pounding of the sea over the years have caused much damage to the village and because of this a storm wall was built to protect it in 1980. The storms were not the only peril that washed up on its shores. Pirates frequented the area many years ago presenting a danger to the local fishermen who have worked from the beaches for hundreds of years. It is said that the sea-borne threat made the fishermen live further inland.

Within the boundaries of Torcross stands the Start Bay Inn, a beautiful 14th century thatched building. It's on the A379 road which runs alongside Slapton Ley and the coast. The road was built in 1856 to provide a link between Kingsbridge and Dartmouth, and two years later a stagecoach service began to run between the two towns. The original road ran between the Inn and the beach which is where the Inn's original facade stood (today the road runs on the opposite side of the building). To pick up or drop off passengers, the coach then went to a set of steps on the side of the building.

Start Bay Inn, Torcross.

The steps are now covered by a small wooden extension but the outline of the original steps can still be seen on the outer wall. The arrival of the stagecoach with mail and passengers would have been quite an event for those small communities such as Torcross and others surrounding it.

On 20th December 1943 Slapton and Torcross were evacuated for D-Day landing practise, referred to as Exercise Tiger. This involved 15,000 allied troops, of which many were young American servicemen. The residents of Torcross were given six weeks to move, and the evacuation of the area lasted for around twelve months. Unfortunately this was to end in tragedy for many of the servicemen involved due to a German e-boat entering the bay causing death to many of the men and destruction to some the training vessels. Forty years later in 1984 Ken Small, author of *The Forgotten Dead* - a book about Exercise Tiger - recovered a Sherman Amphibious Tank under the sea at Slapton. It now stands in the car park opposite the Inn.

I visit the Inn quite regularly and have dined there many times as the food is superb. Sometimes I have had the feeling that there is an energy that exists there and this has led me to speak to Clair who is one of the managers. After speaking to her about the history of the Inn I then asked the question of whether anything unusual had been seen there. I was aware this is not a normal topic of conversation, but I was curious as to what it was that I had sensed on previous visits.

Clair told me that she came to live at the Inn in 1977 when she was five years old, and she lived there for seven or eight years. She admitted that when she was young she felt the place was quite creepy. She told me that something strange had happened to her grandmother who was called Alice and that this was kept from Clair for many years in case it scared her even more. She said that Alice had seen a ghostly little girl in her bedroom, but Clair did not know the full story of what her grandmother had seen. She suggested that I speak to her mother Fay Stubbs to ask her what she remembers about the ghostly encounter. I rang Fay and she gave me the following details.

She recollected that it was around Easter time, April 1984 and that Alice had been ill and was in bed in her bedroom. As Alice awoke and looked about her room she saw that a ghostly little girl was stood looking at her from the bottom of her bed. Alice noticed that the little girl was dressed in very old-fashioned clothes, a small bonnet was on her head and she had on a long dress, which would not have been the fashion in 1984. It was more like Victorian style clothing. As Alice continued to stare at the apparition she noticed that the girl did not appear to be stood on the floor. She was floating in mid-air some inches above the floor. This would be enough to scare the bravest amongst us but the little girl did not seem to mean any harm to Alice and simply turned and smiled at her before disappearing.

Position of the old steps.

The four main characters in this account are Clair, her mother Fay, Fay's mother-in-law Alice and of course the ghost of the young girl. Clair admitted to being scared at times in the Inn, when she was young. It was because of this that she wasn't told of the haunting until some years later and this being the case would not have known to look out for anything unusual occurring in the Inn at that time. It would seem that the apparition was centred on Alice's bedroom at that time and one reason for this I will discuss later.

I feel sure that because Clair was feeling nervous and 'spooked out' that if she had experienced something she would definitely have remembered it. She would have been around the age of twelve when this haunting occurred. Young girls of this age, which is often the onset of puberty, can sometimes be more susceptible to encounters of a paranormal kind. It is a time of innocence and openness which seems to attract paranormal energy. It would seem that this particular ghostly energy was not drawn to Clair or if it was it did not make itself known to her. It is perhaps a good thing that it did not as Clair already felt that there was something creepy about the place. There were times when Clair was older that if she was making a cup of tea and had to carry it upstairs she would only half fill the cup. This was because sometimes when she felt 'spooked' she might shake and she didn't want to spill the tea and also if she wanted to run back down the stairs she could without making too much mess.

Clair's mother Fay was the teller of the tale. This is something that happened approximately 34 years ago. Recalling something from as long back as this can sometimes not be quite as accurate as we think. Our memories can trick us and add or subtract things that may not have happened in quite the way we remember them. Fay seems very clear in her recollection of what happened to Alice, but unfortunately there may be some details, however minor, which might have happened but have not been recollected. For instance, how old did the apparition look? Did she try to speak? Did Alice try to speak to her? How long was she visible for? Did the apparition look distressed? Did Fay feel frightened when she spent time in the Inn after being told the tale?

We are told that Alice was in her bedroom because she had been ill. It is probable that she may have drifted in and out of sleep some of the time. This type of dream state can sometimes make us see some very strange things. They are called hypnagogic hallucinations. This occurs when we are just falling asleep during Stage 1 of NREM (non-rapid eye movement). These hallucinations or visions can seem very real and lead us to believe we are seeing or experiencing things that in reality we are not. In certain circumstances sleep paralysis can occur which can lead us to feel that we cannot move and that 'something' is holding us down.

People who have experienced it say they were gripped with fear and that they felt that a demonic force was out to possess their soul or was trying to crush or smother them. That 'something' is sometimes perceived as a witch, termed 'The Old Hag'. In more severe cases it is perceived as a demon called a Succubus or an Incubus. Another consideration is whether Alice was suffering from a fever or dehydration. We know that she had been unwell so was it a side effect of her illness that made her see what she thought was a little girl? There are a lot of environmental and physiological things to consider when investigating a haunting. Unfortunately because this particular incident happened many years ago there is little evidence to work with. We only have anecdotal evidence and this can sometimes quite innocently be flawed.

The question is, did Alice see a real ghostly little girl in her bedroom or was it due to her illness and sleep deprivation which caused some type of hallucination? Perhaps for years nobody really knew what to think of Alice's story but many years later new evidence was to change this.

The alcove

The alcove where a female ghost has been sighted.

A female spirit has since been seen at the Inn on two separate occasions. The first was in 2017 and witnessed by a customer who was sat quietly talking to another person whilst facing the alcove on the ground floor at the back of the Inn. He saw a female dressed in a long, old-fashioned dress and wearing a bonnet walk across the alcove and disappear. This alcove is in the oldest, original part of the Inn. He turned and said to his colleague "Did you see that?" The colleague quickly turned but didn't see anything.

The way that he described the ghostly apparition with her long, old-fashioned dress and bonnet, was very similar to what Alice described seeing in her bedroom. The age of the female is different but as the ghost moved quickly and was covered in bonnet and long dress it may have influenced his perception of her age. Was this the same ghost that Alice encountered?

The second encounter also occurred in recent years. A man and his wife were running the Inn whilst the landlord and his family were away for a few days. The man went along the landing towards the bathroom and on approaching the door a small girl ran past him causing him to move to one side to let her pass. Initially he thought it was the daughter of the landlord but then remembered that they were away from the Inn and that there was only himself and his wife upstairs. He had to physically move to one side to let her pass as she moved along the corridor.

These two encounters add credence to Alice's tale. They are encounters made at different times by two separate people who knew nothing about the ghostly little girl. It would be nice to have a name for the ghostly little girl but to date I have not been able to clarify who she was. Had she lived at the Inn in the past or was she a passenger on the stagecoach just passing through?

If this ghostly apparition exists, what type of haunting might it be? Considering the small amount of evidence we have to work with I would perhaps consider two types of possible haunting. The first is called Residual Haunting. This type of haunting is probably the most commonly seen, and is witnessed as a type of replay. An example of this is where a figure of a person has been seen to pass by, sometimes only visible from the knee upwards. This is because we are seeing the spirit where it was walking when it was alive and the level of the floor in that area has been raised since that day. It is a replay of something that happened at another time. We can see the apparition but it is totally unaware of our existence. It is like watching a TV show that has already been recorded. There is no interaction because we are in a different time zone.

How this happens is often debated but a popular theory is called The Stone Tape Theory. This is based on the idea that a building is able to absorb a form of energy from living beings during times of high emotional stress. It is thought that the energy can be stored for an unspecific time, and the replay is triggered by someone with the correct attributes, psychic abilities, or even stress levels. It's like a set of psychic videos set on replay. How it actually works is unknown but a theory that is often talked about in paranormal circles is that iron oxide (rust) particles contained in some structures might behave like the iron particles used to store information on video/audio tape. For this to actually happen would involve quite a complex set of things to take place. Also things which are recorded on video/audio tape are in a way focused to one precise place to enable coherent recording. If we say that in the replay theory, recording is absorbed into the fabric of a building then it would be more widespread throughout the fabric which would probably not produce a recording that would be clear enough to reproduce a human figure or voice.

The other type of haunting which may apply to Alice's story is called a classic or traditional haunting. This type of haunting differs from a recording in that it has an intelligence and a will to communicate with an incarnate human being. Alice said that the ghost of the little girl stood near the bottom of her bed and turned and smiled at her. This would suggest that the ghost was aware of Alice's presence whereas a residual haunting would not have even seen her. This type of haunting can sometimes result in doors being banged, cupboard doors flying open, strange noises or odours. It is thought there is a wish to communicate through different methods. It can also produce cold spots and affect electrical appliances.

The sighting of the woman in the long dress and bonnet, seen in the alcove of the Inn is quite interesting. Was it the same ghost of the young girl that Alice saw in her bedroom? The man who saw the ghost described it as a "woman in an old fashioned long dress, wearing a bonnet". He also said that he only got a quick glimpse of the woman. Whether this ghostly female was the same young girl that Alice saw we cannot be sure. Alice said that it was a young girl that she saw in her bedroom but the female seen in later years by the man downstairs appears to have been older. The man said that he only caught a glimpse of her as she walked through the alcove. The height of the apparition may have led him to believe it was an older woman and he may have been right.

On the other hand what if the apparition was the same young female ghost who was levitating above ground level like the one in Alice's bedroom. She would appear to be taller and that could make one believe she was older than she actually was. Although she was levitating above the floor when Alice saw her she was close enough to Alice for her to see that the ghost had young female features. So although the ghost would have appeared to be quite tall Alice could see that she was only young, whilst the one seen in the alcove was at a distance away and moved quickly out of sight therefore making it difficult to distinguish her age. It is difficult to come to a conclusion as to whether these sightings may have been of the same ghost. It could be that the ghost seen in the alcove may be that of another female spirit. Whether this ghost was purely residual energy we do not know as it did not interact with its surroundings and was not challenged in any way which would have helped to determine what type of energy it was.

When Alice told family members what she had seen in her bedroom they were at a loss as to why the ghostly young girl was not standing on the ground but seemed to be levitating some way above it. The answer to the mystery became clear when the outline of some steps were noticed on the outside of the building. These steps are now covered in by a wooden structure but on the outer wall we can see the outline of the steps where they would have been years ago when the stagecoach visited the Inn. These would be the same steps that people would use to climb on and off the stagecoach and the top of the steps align with Alice's bedroom. This then made sense as to why the ghostly girl appeared to be hovering above the floor level. Alice would have been seeing her where she was stood years ago on a level with the steps.

The sighting by the man who was staying at the Inn was quite strange. He said that he was just about to enter the bathroom when a young girl walked past him and along the corridor. He was so sure of what he was seeing that he actually moved to one side to let her pass. This would suggest that the apparition was perceived to be quite solid and what may be termed as Corporeal (physical form).

This is a more unusual form of apparition as they are usually seen as Incorporeal (without a physical body). They may have the appearance of a person but are quite often seen as shadows, luminous or transparent. It is uncertain as to whether this man had any previous knowledge about the female apparitions connected to the Inn. If he did he may have felt a little uneasy at times but it would be unlikely that he would have had the experience that befell him. He might have attributed the odd noise or shadow to something 'spooky' but to move aside for something physically walking past him is very different.

He stated that at the time he thought it was the daughter of the landlord and then he remembered that the landlord and his family were not in the building. That would suggest that in his mind he felt he was in a normal situation moving aside to let a young lady go past. It was only after she had passed by him that he then remembered that this was impossible, suggesting that he was not expecting anything ghostly, adding to the credibility of his story.

Conclusion

The Start Bay Inn is a very interesting case. It appears to be haunted by a young female and possibly by an older female depending on the interpretation of the female seen in the alcove on the ground floor of the Inn.

The types of possible hauntings range from residual energy to intelligent energy and also a corporeal encounter, although it seems odd that if a ghost is seen as corporeal that they are able to pass through solid objects such as walls.

All the sightings have been female in nature and so far no male or other types of activity have been experienced. The young female ghost is interesting and probably more of an intelligent or classical haunting rather than a residual energy. If it was a residual energy it would not be able to interact with her environment, it would appear as a spirit but would periodically repeat the same movements as though a replay button has been pressed on a recorder. Whether it is the spirit of a female connected with the Inn in some way or whether it is connected to the stage coach that used to call in at the Inn is also unknown. I contacted a curatorial assistant at the Kingsbridge Cookworthy Museum which is local to the Inn, who kindly searched back through files and books to check if there was any information about a child's death at the Inn or any ghostly disturbances in the past. Unfortunately without a name or short date range they have been unable to find any information that might throw a light on who the female might be.

It would have been nice to know the name of the ghost that haunts the Start Bay Inn, it is an intriguing mystery.

Start Bay Inn - comparison grid

		Bedroom	Alcove	Landing
Encounter	Characteristics	girl little	female	girl small
	Activity	standing above the floor looking at witness	walking disappeared	running
	Description	bonnet small dress long old-fashioned	bonnet dress long old-fashioned	
Witness	Characteristics	female middle-aged	male	male
	Activity	lying ill	sitting talking	walking
	Date	1984 April	2017	recent years (at 2018)

A summary analysis of the several sightings at the Start Bay Inn.

Market Street, Dartmouth

Market Street takes its name from the old pannier market which dates back to 1828. In the early days ponies carried goods to the market on their backs every day in baskets (panniers) full of fresh farm produce, to be sold to the local people of the town. Today it's still a lively and vibrant place, with a wide range of artisan goods as well as fresh produce, tempting cafes and bric-a-brac stalls.

Market Street.

In the autumn of 1983 Mandy Campbell stayed for a few days at a house in Market Street that belonged to her boyfriend's parents. One night she was woken in the small hours by the sound of a muffled alarm apparently coming from her room.

Mandy got up and searched until, on the mantelpiece, she found a china tankard, inside of which a digital watch was sounding its alarm.

The watch displayed the time 02:00, which is a curious time to want an alarm call. The clock bell of nearby St Saviour's church rang out, chiming two o'clock, confirming the time.

The watch looked like one of the first popular digital watches that dated to the 1970s. Mandy managed to find how to turn the alarm off, and went back to bed.

Just as she was drifting off to sleep again, she heard the sound of footsteps across the floor of the attic room above. This immediately "put her hackles up" as she knew for a fact that the room was so stuffed with used furniture that she said "you couldn't get a 'fag-paper' between it and it would have been impossible to walk across."

The footsteps continued down the stairs and stopped outside the door of her room. She could hear breathing but no other movement, and nothing else happened. Even so, she was pretty scared by this time and couldn't go back to sleep.

About half an hour later the footsteps started again, but didn't continue. Mandy said "I fleetingly thought I might be able to go back to sleep after the footsteps had stopped so I turned over in bed pulled the covers over my ears and closed my eyes, but within two minutes of me doing that a very loud rapping sound started to come from the skirting board about a foot away from my face."

At this point she became rigid with fear. The rapping went on for about an hour, on and off. Just when she thought it had stopped, it started again. The memories of that night remain vivid in her memory.

"I could see that there was nobody in the room because the street light shone through the curtains making everything visible. I didn't sleep for the rest of the night and when I asked everyone in the morning, nobody else had heard a thing."

Then she learned that the watch, which belonged to her boyfriend, had broken a couple of years earlier, and hadn't worked since.

Mandy's story began almost humorously, with a trivial incident that nevertheless bears the hallmark of the remarkable coincidence (the synchronisation between the mysteriously revived watch and the church clock). What followed made for a very uncomfortable night indeed: footsteps approaching in the dead of night, the presence of a stranger lingering outside the bedroom door, the sound of heavy breathing...

For a young woman in a strange house, that's practically the stuff of nightmare. And some readers might suppose that's all it was. But that wouldn't be entirely fair. It is true that when considering whether a place may be haunted, parapsychologists need to take account of certain environmental effects such as the natural creaking and tapping noises made by pipes or wood contracting when the heating is turned off, which may explain the disturbance otherwise reputed to be evidence of a restless spirit.

When we are in our own homes we get used to the everyday noises that the house makes, but when we're in a different place, somewhere we've never stayed in before, every sound is new to us, and their causes are unknown, putting us mentally on alert. This is called the New House Effect. The more we listen, the more we hear, and the more sleep-deprived we can become. It's a vicious cycle because the more anxious and scared we become, the more our bodies release adrenalin, preparing us for instantaneous fight or flight. But when you're lying in bed, where can you run? And how can you fight a ghost?

But in Mandy's account, the way the experience followed a script that led the footsteps across the upstairs room, down the stairs and to her door, is difficult to ascribe to random creaks in the woodwork, and the sheer intensity of the rapping at the climax is hard to explain away.

The way Mandy appears to have been deliberately woken, is another striking feature of this experience. Without that peculiar wake up call, she may simply have slept through the quiet beginnings of the footsteps, and without that storyline, the noises in the skirting may, in isolation, have been put down to the New House Effect.

Disturbances at Dartmouth

Some very strange events happened between 1996 and 1998 in a private residence in Dartmouth. The person who related this tale to me lived there for just over two years and during that time shared the residence with various flatmates. Strange things would start to happen when a new flatmate took residence - furniture would be moved, noises were heard and an apparition of a lady was sometimes seen.

One afternoon the flatmate invited a friend round. Whilst they were talking the friend suddenly asked if there was a piece of paper and a pen. When questioned as to why she needed this, she said she could 'see' a ghostly lady. The flatmate could not see anything but her friend could and set about drawing what she could 'see'.

She drew a lady of about fifty years of age, quite plump, and wearing some sort of old-fashioned uniform. The uniform was navy blue with big buttons, and included a mop hat and an apron.

She also said that the lady was smiling and did not appear to be menacing or scary in any way. Her height was from the floor up to the height of the light switch, which would probably not be very tall. After this had occurred investigations were made at Dartmouth Museum as to what this uniform might be. It was thought that it could be the clothes of a dairy maid.

One morning, the bookcase that was usually up against the wall, was discovered to have been moved. Not only had it moved, but the books that it contained had been placed in piles on the floor. These books were heavy cookery books and directories, volumes that had quite a lot of weight to them. This must have happened during the night or early morning and yet nothing had been heard. Neither of the residents accepted responsibility for moving the bookcase or the books.

Loud bangs were sometimes heard between the hours of 4am and 6am, apparently emanating from the sitting room wall. This may tie in with the theory that the apparition was that of a dairy maid, as milking would have probably taken place around this time.

The teller of this strange tale did not feel frightened whilst living there as the ghostly dairy maid looked quite happy and nothing threatening happened. One thing though was a little unsettling - one morning, whilst awakening from sleep there was a feeling of something heavy, pressing down, which prevented the movement of arms or legs. Apparently this has not happened since, just on this one occasion whilst living in this particular residence.

This phenomenon has been reported many times in different locations by many people. When it occurs it is very frightening as its victim is quite unable to move. In folk-lore it is known as The Old Hag or Witch. It was thought that she would come and sit on your chest to hold you down and frighten you. In the modern scientific world it's called sleep-paralysis and it's thought this happens when we're just coming out of sleep and the brain becomes active before the body 'wakes up'. This gives the sensation of being physically held down.

Thankfully the person who related this story to me has now moved and enjoys a peaceful life in a new residence.

The Spinning Wheel Café and Tea Rooms, Dartmouth

Reputedly one of the oldest Tea Rooms in Devon, the Spinning Wheel Café (Hauley Road) is in the heart of Dartmouth. Here gourmet coffee, delicious food and cream teas are served daily, and customers come to enjoy the food and ambiance of the building, but it would seem that some visitors have never left.

There have been several sightings of ghostly customers in the past and it would seem that some of these apparitions are very mischievous. In spring 2017 Wendy, the manager of the café, told me that on the whole things have been fairly quiet in recent years, but a strange thing did happen to one female member of staff.

Wendy recalled an occasion when a waitress was carrying a tray through to the café when a knife slipped from the tray and landed on the floor. A thorough search was carried out but the knife could not be found. They knew the knife must be somewhere on the floor and so had another good look around. Eventually the knife was found lying on the floor in between two cupboards.

As the knife was being retrieved, a few butter pats (pre-wrapped, small individual servings of butter) were also found on the floor behind the cupboard. On removing the kick-board at the front of the cupboard they found hundreds of pats of butter lying on the floor beneath the unit. The pats had not been marked in any way and they didn't have any teeth marks in them to suggest being put there by any animal.

There was a large amount of pats, enough to fill a black bin liner, a process witnessed by a customer in the café. Wendy added "There was no way for the pats to have fallen there accidentally as they are stored in the fridge in another room."

It is difficult to make a comment as to how these pats of butter came to be hidden under the unit, especially in view of the sheer quantity of pats involved. I suggested to Wendy that over time the pats may have dropped behind the cupboard accidentally, but she didn't think that this was the case as the cupboard fits snuggly to the wall.

The cupboard (the highlights are from the window).

Were they apported there? An apport is when something physical is transferred from one place to another by a spirit. Although this has never been proven to happen when scientifically challenged, there are many anecdotal stories of it happening.

On another occasion Wendy was working near the kitchen window and thought she saw someone pass by. Thinking that it might be one of the staff she checked, but there was no one there.

Quite often we hear reports of ghostly sightings that have been seen by peripheral or side vision. These are sightings that are not seen by our central vision but are just caught 'in the corner of the eye.' When we see things with our peripheral vision it is something that is out of our central area of focus and so is not seen clearly. Peripheral vision is good at detecting movement but not so good at definition, so it is often quite difficult to get an accurate impression of what we have seen.

Nethway House, Kingswear

I received an invitation from Lynne Maurer to visit Nethway House, Kingswear. Lynne is one of the present owners, and had previously mentioned to me that some strange things had happened at the house, and asked if I'd like to take a look for myself.

So on 18th October 2018, on a bright autumnal day I set off to Kingswear. After driving down the road to Dartmouth I saw the turn-off for Nethway and made my way along the lane. Presently I saw the sign for Nethway House and turned into the long driveway which winds its way up to the front of the large mansion house. Two large ornate lions stand guard either side of the entrance door.

Lynne's daughter Victoria came out to meet me followed by Lynne who welcomed me with a smile. I followed them into the kitchen area and was greeted by Lynne's cats who looked at me with suspicion and perhaps a little irritation for disturbing their afternoon sleep.

One of the big cat guardians of Nethway House.

Nethway House is a Grade II listed building, built in the fashionable William and Mary style around the end of the 17th century. It is steeped in history and sits amongst eight hectares (twenty acres) of beautiful gardens and fields.

An earlier house had stood on the site, but was burned down. It had dated back to the late 1300s and may have also had a chapel.

Nethway House.

It is said that on 23rd July 1671 King Charles II visited and slept here before journeying to Exeter the next day, but the claim hasn't yet been independently verified. There is a tree in the grounds that was planted by H.R.H. Prince George on 2nd November 1878.

During the Second World War children from the city of Plymouth were relocated to various places for their safety and some were sent to stay at Nethway House. The house became the temporary home to hundreds of children while the war raged on.

Apart from the interesting history of the house it may also be what is known as a Calendar House. That is a house that architecturally symbolises the months, days, weeks and season in a year. It has four chimneys which represent the four seasons, twelve bedrooms which represent the months of the year, fifty-two windows for the weeks in a year and possibly the panes of glass may amount to the days in a year. The theme for this type of house dates back to the Elizabethan era when it was the fashion amongst the gentry to showcase any advance made in science and especially mathematics in as unique a way as was possible. This is how the idea of building a house which encompassed the components of a year became popular, although there weren't many of these houses built. There also appears to be a passageway which runs under the house and is thought to terminate at Man Sands which is 1.9 miles (3km) away. Part of the tunnel has given way and so it was blocked off some years ago as it was unsafe. If the tunnel does go to Man Sands was it used by smugglers years ago? No evidence of that has been found but it is an interesting thought.

Nethway House has a history of hauntings. There is a story about a young woman many years ago, who was employed as a nursery maid for the family who lived there at that time. The family's son took a liking to the maid and one day took his feelings a little too far and the poor maid became pregnant. It appeared that the son did not want anything to do with the maid which left the poor girl in a terrible predicament. With no one to help or turn to she climbed out onto the roof of the house (or perhaps she went to a window) and jumped to her death. It is said that she was not buried in the churchyard but was hastily buried somewhere on the owner's land. To this day her grave has not been found.

When Lynne first came to live at the house she decided to make a few alterations to some of the rooms. She was very shocked and surprised to find that a line of salt had been left under the skirting of the outer wall of one of the rooms. It has been suggested in the past that an exorcism was performed on the house, possibly in the 1960s. An exorcism is usually performed on a person who is thought to be possessed by evil spirits, and is intended to drive the evil spirit out of the person and return them to normality. But an exorcism can also be carried out on a building, as a house cleansing. This is usually because the spirit that is thought to be haunting the property is bringing unrest to the people living there. During the exorcism/cleansing, salt is used as a sign of purification and a protection barrier against the spirit entering the property again. It may be that the line of salt that Lynne found was originally used for the cleansing and had been left there as a protection for the house.

As Lynne took me on a walk around the house she told me that mainly on the upper floor of the building she had seen lights which were a bluish colour. These were not domestic lights, these were more like orb lights which moved about. Sometimes room lights were found to have been switched on by themselves as no one in the house had turned them on. The radio had also turned on at odd times.

There are two main staircases in the house and it was on one of these staircases that Lynne sensed someone moving. When she turned to look there was no one there. She has also heard her name being called by what sounded like a female voice and she was so convinced that someone had called her that she answered them, but again, there was no one there.

In the entrance lobby area of the house Lynne used to have a display of her collection of porcelain dolls. Eventually she had to move them because they kept getting moved about mysteriously. None of the family had touched them.

Richard Westlake is a gardener on the estate and has worked there for many years. He told me that his mother - Anne Westlake - lived in one of the cottages attached to the side of the main house, and worked in the main house in the early 1980s.

She said she thought she'd seen a ghostly lady, and one day felt someone follow her down the main staircase (the same staircase where Lynne had also sensed someone behind her).

Richard went on to say that some days he can't work on the water garden. I asked him exactly what he meant and he said it is as though something does not want him there. He just feels that he cannot work there and yet on other days it is fine.

The water garden.

In the row of cottages where Anne used to live, doors have been heard closing and in one of them the indentation of a body was left on the top of a bed which had just been made and was not there before.

Whilst I was talking to Richard, Lynne took me to one side and showed me an area laid to lawn where she saw a ghostly lady walk along and disappear into the wooded garden beyond it.

Lawn where a ghostly lady appeared.

Victoria, Lynne's daughter told me about things that had often occurred in and around her room. She said that when the decorator was in the room he heard someone coming up the stairs. He called out and told them not open the door as he was behind it painting. He thought it was someone bringing him a cup of tea, but when he got down from his ladder and opened the door, no one was there.

She said that there was one time when she had mislaid the lens cover from her camera and looked all over the room for it and could not find it anywhere. Eventually she gave up and went to bed. In the morning the missing lens cover was placed right in the centre of the rug next to her bed where she'd be sure to find it.

Victoria had some friends stay over and their room was next to hers. She said all was well until during the night the friends felt something rattling the headboard. When they opened their eyes they got the fright of their lives, they saw a ghostly little boy hovering, crossed-legged next to the bed. They ran out of the room and slept in Victoria's room for the rest of night.

On another occasion a female friend of Victoria's stayed over in the same bedroom as the previous two friends. She settled down for the night and after a while had the sensation that her hair was being moved on the side of her face which was upper-most on the pillow. It was as though something wanted her to listen and was moving the hair out of the way. She woke up feeling very scared. At this point, Buddy, Victoria's black cat, came into the room and sat with her as if to protect and comfort her, and stayed with her for the rest of the night.

Buddy the little cat guardian.

Sometimes Victoria has sensed someone standing in the doorway of her room. Buddy seems to sense it as well and goes over to sit with Victoria as if to protect her. Buddy is a beautiful cat with large green eyes. It's as though he has a human soul and he seems to be very protective not only of Victoria, but of others as well. He is almost like an animal talisman or good luck charm who senses when something is wrong or someone is scared.

Victoria has also seen orbs in the upper room, which unlike the ones that Lynne saw which were blue, these are golden in colour. She experienced a ghostly encounter with a lady who was seen in a doorway and was also seen in the area upstairs. She could see the outline of a shape which was moving and which was also golden in colour.

Nethway House is very interesting. Whilst I was walking round the building with Lynne and Victoria I sensed various areas that seemed to have an energy connected to them. None of the energies felt bad or malevolent, in fact, one of the energies felt very mischievous, as though belonging to a child. Whether this was from the little boy who has been seen there, I am not sure, but he may be the one who is responsible for moving things and turning lights on and off, moving Lynne's dolls about.

It is a type of poltergeist activity when things are physically moved but so far it does not seem to have caused many problems. As I entered the room where Victoria's friends had had disturbed nights, I immediately sensed a strong energy. This was before I knew what had been happening in there, so it had not influenced me in any way. Victoria said that sometimes when she is in there it has felt icy cold, more so than in the rest of the house.

The other ghostly sightings are possibly mainly residual energy - a replay of events or people who have lived there in the past, recorded somehow. We can see them but they're not aware of us.

The area that is known as the water garden is quite interesting as it's thought to be the area where the nursery maid may have landed when she fell from the window/roof. There is a theory that water may have the ability to act as a battery for storing spirit energy. There is a theory that it has the capability of memory, as in Homeopathy. Is it possible that the water is somehow transferring a feeling of sadness or death when environmental conditions are right and the gardener Richard has been experiencing this?

We don't really know, and perhaps we are not supposed to know the answer to some of these things. Such mysteries make any study of the paranormal endlessly fascinating.

Poltergeist Activity, Dartmouth

When David Drury and his brother commenced work at Warfleet Cottage they had no idea what lay in store for them. It was in the 1990s when David, his brother and a fellow carpenter started work on the cottage. They started their day like any other, chatting and setting tools out to start the rebuilding and decorating work.

After a busy morning's work they made their way to the kitchen and sat down for a hard earned rest and tea-break. Suddenly the clock on the wall lifted off and shot across the kitchen, made a right turn, and crashed down the hall.

They all looked at each other, totally shocked at what they'd all witnessed. They tried to think of a reason how that could have happened but couldn't. After a somewhat subdued tea-break they continued with their work.

Halfway through the morning David's brother was walking through the hallway when a hammer flew past his head. He shouted to the carpenter to be more careful, but when he went to check he found him outside, talking to the next door neighbour.

David and his brother completed their work, and they left the carpenter to finish fitting a new window.

When they all met up the next day the carpenter said that about 10pm the front door opened and he heard footsteps crossing the floor. The carpenter thought one of the brothers had returned and he called out their names but received no reply. After going down the stairs there was no one there but there was a smell of stale beer. With that the carpenter packed up his things and promptly left the cottage.

The following morning David talked to the neighbour and he learned something of the history of the area. There had been a pottery here and before that, in the 1800s, a brewery. The brewery manager had met with a tragic and fatal accident, and his ghost haunted the cottages. He had been crushed to death by a beer vat, which could have accounted for the smell noticed by the carpenter. Unfortunately the neighbour cannot provide any more details as he too has sadly since passed away.

After receiving this story from David I rang him to thank him for sharing his story with me. He told me that alongside the pottery, which is the larger of the buildings and the one that used to be the brewery in the mid-1800s, is a row of three or four cottages and it was in one of these that David and his brother were working when the incidents occurred. The poltergeist activity mainly seemed to be occurring whilst the cottage was being worked on, and once the work was finished, this appeared to stop.

The old pottery building was converted for residential use early in the 21st century, but in the 19th century it had seen service as a paper mill, a corn mill, as well as a brewery - the latter having a number of different managers over the years. During the Second World War, incidentally, it was occupied by British Commandos, after which it became Dartmouth Pottery.

My research into the history of the cottages and mill unearthed no mention of a death at the brewery but when big casks of beer were daily being loaded on and off large drays it is possible that accidents may happen as a result. Whatever is haunting the cottages would seem to be at rest again, perhaps until further renovations disturb the peace once more.

The Church of St Petrox, Dartmouth

In June 2015 Wendy Birchall was on holiday in Devon with her sister and friend and decided it would be nice to have a look inside St Petrox church before having a look at the neighbouring castle. What happened next was a shock to all three of them.

The beautiful church of St Petrox lies to the south of the town and is one of three ancient churches in Dartmouth. Deeds relating to 'Little Dartmouth', dating back to 1192, are possibly where we find the first mention of this religious building.

The church lies adjacent to the castle and is a Grade 1 listed building, and was practically rebuilt around 1641. It may have originally been a primitive chapel with a holy well, which came to be known as the Monastery of St Peter. Today it provides a particularly romantic and beautiful setting for weddings for the residents of Dartmouth.

Wendy recalled that it was around 2.30pm when they had looked around the outside of the church and then decided to have a look inside. On entering the church they began to look at the inscriptions on the old plaques and other memorials.

Wendy and her friend had stopped to look at the memorial to Elizabeth and Edward Roope and their son Edward (who died respectively, in 1683, 1689 and 1674). They began to

The memorial to the Roope family.

discuss how surreal it felt that the bones of those people were actually in the church. It was at this point that a pencil flew through the air and hit Wendy.

There was no one else in the church at the time only Wendy's sister and friend and they certainly didn't throw the pencil as they were by Wendy's side. Wendy recalls "the pencil basically gently flew through the air and hit me but not with any real force. We were all astounded by it and could offer no explanation."

She also said that only a few minutes earlier she had been standing in the pulpit and wondered if perhaps a 'spirit' had taken exception to that. It was two or three minutes after stepping down that the pencil hit her.

The pulpit.

She wondered about keeping the pencil because she had just said a prayer for lost loved ones and she thought that it might be a sign from her late father. She said "It was very weird. I also find white feathers all the time, as I believe in spirit." A white feather is often thought to be the sign of the presence of an angel.

It was a very strange thing to happen, especially inside a church. Whether it was a spirit who felt angry at Wendy for standing inside the pulpit we may never know. She had just offered a prayer for loved ones and was thinking about her father and asking for a 'sign', and perhaps that is was exactly what she got and the pencil was the sign. It is difficult not to wonder what might be drawn or written with such a special instrument.

The vicar of St Petrox is Father Will Hazelwood who is the vicar of the United Benefice of Dartmouth and Dittisham. I contacted Fr Will and he told me that the church is still used regularly for Christian worship and that it relies entirely on the congregation and visitors' kindness to provide donations which help to keep the church watertight and maintained.

The Church of St Petrox nestles among the towers of Dartmouth Castle.

Haunting at Slapton Sands

Slapton Sands is famously, or infamously perhaps, where a rehearsal for the D-Day landings went tragically wrong. Exercise Tiger (often but inaccurately called Operation Tiger) lasted from 22nd to 30th April 1944, and was one of many in the local area during the preparations for D-Day.

The wholesale evacuation of part of the South Hams had been ordered to allow American servicemen to practice at Slapton for the planned landing at 'Utah Beach', Normandy. Around 1:30am on Friday 28th April, German torpedo boats in Start Bay attacked an Allied training convoy heading for Slapton. 749 US soldiers and sailors were killed or reported missing in action.

On the anniversary of that deadly event, in 2009, Dawn Lodge visited the site and drew several portraits apparently of American servicemen who lost their lives there. Dawn is a psychic artist who attempts to communicate with spirit and is able to draw an impression of what she sees. She had been invited to visit Slapton Sands by members of the Hidden Realms Paranormal Team in an attempt to add some faces to the spirit energy that has often been said to be trapped there.

One of several portraits drawn by psychic artist Dawn Lodge at Slapton Sands.

Hidden Realms had a history of involvement with Slapton Sands and had mounted an investigation there the previous year.

Just before midnight on the chilly evening of Sunday 27th April 2008, four investigators gathered at the Strete end of the beach: Dennis and Betty Hemmings, a guest who had accompanied the group before and who also had a good knowledge of ship construction, and myself, the author.

We parked our cars in the car-park and walked down to a stretch of beach to which we all felt drawn, and waited for the early hours of Monday 28th April.

It was a very cold night and we must have looked a strange sight, four shivering people just sitting on the sands. Around 2am I began to 'link in' (by this I mean I appeared to receive communication from spirit) to a man on a ship.

He was in a room with lots of shelves stacked with blankets and boxes. In fact, all sorts of items were stacked everywhere. This seemed to be the area he was connected with. I could also 'see' a table which had seating down one side of it. The table was empty but its contents, which looked like metal plates and cups, seemed to be scattered about. I asked our guest if these would be the types of utensils that would have been used and he verified that they would.

I asked for the man's name and was given the name Stevie Stephenson (it sounded a bit like Sanderson) from Illinois.

Images of male spirits drawn by a psychic artist.

He seemed to be very anxious about something that was stored in a lower area of the boat which contained something to do with the landing. I also asked for the name of the ship and was shown a large letter T followed by a small letter or digit.

The link weakened and we walked to another part of the beach and tried once again to link in. This time I was given the name of Archie Andrews. It seemed as though this man was in respiratory distress and was in great pain each time he breathed in. It was as though he had inhaled smoke/fumes which burned his lungs. I was then shown an engine room full of smoke.

The next link I was given was when a group of men (in spirit) stood before me. One of them held a large book which had a rigid cover and a ringed metal spine. He held this book out to me and I was given this message "Remember us, don't forget us." I was given the impression that this book contained the names and addresses of many men who had lost their lives, but were still unaccounted for. They wanted their families to know where they were (their remains) and how they had died.

I then lost the link. At that point we decided to head home as it was a bitterly cold night.

The next day I received a phone call from the guest who had accompanied us on the vigil that night. He had gone through some of the records on the internet and had found that six Quartermaster units sustained losses due to enemy action during training for the D-Day Invasion. The 3206th Quartermaster Service Company sustained the heaviest losses of any unit during the night of 27th to 28th April 1944. This may be the reason that I saw this man in a room containing lots of supplies.

With reference to the name of Stevie Stephenson/Sanderson, Dennis had a look at the US federal government website (ABMC) and found that James W. Stephenson, Private First Class, US Army, 3206th Quartermaster Service Company, died 28th April 1944, missing in action. The forename doesn't match the one I was given but it is possible he was known as Stevie, a nickname derived from his surname.

Dennis had a look at the reported casualty figures and there appeared to be a deficit of those accounted for. Could this be what the men with the book were trying to tell us? Despite repeated assurances from the authorities about the final burial place of those who perished in the Exercise Tiger tragedy at Start Bay, many people remain unconvinced. If some of these unaccounted men were buried in the Slapton Area, where were they buried?

I was curious to try an experiment at home to see if I could locate the whereabouts of their bodies. I tried a type of remote viewing and concentrated on an area where the men might be buried. I was guided to draw a field, with a wooden farm gate at the right hand side of it situated at the end of a long hedge. On the opposite side of the field there was a long line of tall trees. The right hand side of the field faced the sea. I then placed the map into an envelope and gave it to Dennis to keep.

Some days later Dennis was told of a place, by a lady who was originally from the Slapton area, where she believed the bodies to be buried. Dennis, Betty and I then drove to the area. When Dennis stopped the car I looked out of the window and saw what looked like the field that I had drawn. Dennis opened the envelope and saw that everything was correct except there were no trees. We concluded that my map must be wrong.

When Dennis saw the lady again she asked how we had got on, and Dennis said that the layout of the map seemed to be right but there were no trees. She explained that many years ago there were elm trees there and they became rotten with Dutch Elm disease and had to be cut down. So perhaps the map was right and I had drawn it as it would have been at the time of Exercise Tiger.

There is an argument for allowing the dead to rest in peace, wherever they're interred, but the American military has a proclaimed policy of bringing all such missing in action back to native soil.

After the initial investigation there seemed to be continual synchronicities connected with Exercise Tiger. Is this spirit contact or coincidence? Synchronicity is a term coined by the psychologist Carl Jung to denote events that are not linked by any immediate instance of cause and effect, but which appear to have a significant connection due to the coincidence of their timing. There are those who consider it to be a figment of the imagination, while others consider it to be a message sent by spirit.

Some notes of my synchronicities about this matter:

- ❖ 28th April 2008: Hidden Realms investigation at Slapton Sands.

- ❖ 30th April 2008. An elderly patient that I was looking after in the hospital told me he'd been involved with "the goings on" at Slapton Sands. He was a Quartermaster in the Land Army based in Yorkshire. I asked his son about this and his son said that he was never based here in Devon, only Yorkshire. Later the son came back to me and said that there was a "length of time when no one knows where his father was whilst he was in the army." Was he involved with the Slapton Incident in some way? Apparently the men were sworn to secrecy.

- ❖ 6th May 2008. I was on duty in the hospital and had a look in the book-box, a place where patients leave books so that others can read them. There was nothing that interested me and I walked off to the staff room. After a few minutes I came out of the staff room and passed the book-box again. Standing up at the back of the box was a large book entitled *D-Day: The Dramatic Story of the World's Greatest Invasion*, by Dan Parry. That book was not there before. Of course a patient may have been looking at the book and returned it whilst I was in the staff room. If that is what happened, were they led by spirit to return it at that particular time for a reason. Was that reason because I needed to see it and pick it up? The book is noticeably above average in size, so it's very unlikely I could simply have missed seeing it.

- ❖ 11th July 2008. I went to Ways with Words (a literary event) at Dartington Hall to attend a talk given by Kate Mosse the author of *Labyrinth and Sepulchre*. Whilst there I went to the book fair which is upstairs in one of the old buildings. As I got to the top of the stairs I looked across at the second-hand book stall where each year I spend a long time browsing, and a book was propped up against a shelf facing me. As I walked over to it I saw it was about an American student who writes a thesis about the incident at Slapton Sands. She comes over to England and stays near Slapton and becomes stalked by a spirit who is somehow tied in with the incident. Okay, could be a coincidence, but the theme of the story sounds slightly familiar and I am sure that there can't be many fictional books which have the Slapton Incident as their main theme. Was I meant to see it?

❖ 18th July 2008. Whilst at George Best Belfast City Airport, I decided to pass a bit of time by going into the bookshop. I walked through the door and up to a shelf, and there is yet another book with the letters D-Day in large print facing me.

❖ 5th August 2008. I visited Berry Pomeroy and was lucky enough to find the church open. I had a good look around and found a particular tomb I was interested in, and wrote down the information I needed. Whilst in the church I noticed that a small display had been set up on a table top. I decided to go and have a look at it. It was dedicated to all the American servicemen who lost their lives in the D-Day rehearsals, some of whom had been stationed at nearby villages. There was a list of names and some photographs, a commemoration of the men who died. Was I meant to see this as a reminder by the group of men in spirit who showed me the book whilst on the Slapton investigation?

❖ Somewhere about this time I decided to spend some time at home trying to link-in with those men to see if I could gain any more information that may help to identify them. I was shown a field which is laid out in a particular way and which had some tall trees at the back of it (this was the map I drew, referred to above).

❖ 26th August 2008. Dennis, Betty, and I decide to go back to Slapton and spend some time linking-in to spirit.

❖ 2nd September 2008. I went to visit a friend of mine who lives at Moretonhampstead. She knew about the various investigations that we had been doing, and said she had a couple of books that I might find helpful, one being Ken Small's book: *The Forgotten Dead*. I decided that I didn't want to read through either of those books at this time as it may colour my thoughts about what happened at Slapton and give me information that I didn't want for obvious reasons. BUT having said that I did look at the list of chapters and saw one entitled The Missing Graves. This I decided to have a brief look at in case it mentioned the field which I had drawn. I had a look at the last page of that chapter and a sentence caught my attention. It was Ken Small talking about the possibility of the missing dead soldiers being found and exhumed. He said that he did not want this to happen. That got me thinking that perhaps I should just leave well alone and respect his wishes. He had done so much to bring to light what had happened that night at Slapton in 1944 and I had the idea that perhaps I have been shown this particular sentence to put an end to my recent train of thought. It was a difficult decision, part of me wanted to find out what had happened to these lost men, but then if any of them were to be found there would have to be repatriation and involvement from their families. Would it be better to leave things well alone as it was so many years ago and a degree of acceptance now established by the families?

- ❖ 17th September 2008. I went into a supermarket in Torquay to do some shopping. A couple of people were chatting about everyday issues. I couldn't help but overhear them as I passed by. As I walked away the man said suddenly in a very loud voice "if you go back about fifty years ago to the D-Day landings..." I stopped in my tracks and just blanked it out. When I got home I sat and relaxed with the local newspaper the *Herald Express* to see what had been happening in the area, and what do I see on the page "Emotional trip back for D-Day Veterans". When will it stop!?

❖ 15th January 2010. Tonight I received a phone call from a lady who wanted to speak to me about the spirits that had been sensed at Slapton Sands. Dennis had given her my phone number early last year but she had not rung me at that time. She was most surprised that she had in fact rung me by mistake this evening as she thought she had rung someone else and got me instead. I nearly dropped the phone because I thought, here we go again! Synchronicities, it keeps coming back to me. Why or how did she end up ringing my number when she had not meant to? She told me that she and a friend had been to visit Slapton in October 2008 and had helped a number of American men whose spirits may have remained trapped where they died, to move on to a higher realm where they hopefully found peace.

When Hidden Realms carried out the initial vigil on 28th April 2008 I mentioned that we were given the name of Stevie Stevenson and that he seemed to be on board a ship. There was also a group of men who came forward with a book, which I have described earlier in this story. I have sometimes thought that these men seemed somehow different to the ones on board the ship. As though from different situations.

There has been talk in the past that there was a disaster on 27th April 1944 when American troops were killed by their own side in a friendly fire incident. As the troops ran to the shore from landing craft they were mown down by their comrades who were acting as German defenders, and using live ammunition instead of blanks. It is alleged that the number of men who were killed in this incident was kept secret and simply added to the number who died in the E-boat attack the next day. These claims have always been denied by those in power, but local people witnessed mass graves being dug, as reported in *The Guardian* (Townsend 2004).

Was it this group of men who came forward in spirit connected to this training incident and not the E-boat disaster? They had wanted their families to know what had happened to them. If they died in the alleged training disaster then their spirits may feel aggrieved and want the truth to be known.

Ghostly Encounter with a Cream Cake, Dartmouth

Rinaldo Gozdek had a very strange encounter with an angry ghost whilst staying at his aunt's home in Townstal. It was in 2003 and he had decided to take a walk into the town to look for a special treat. It was not for him, it was for Aunty. He wanted to buy her a little gift just to say 'thank-you' and he decided that a nice cake would be something she would enjoy. It was not to be just an ordinary cake, he wanted to buy a nice large one, topped with cream, which he knew she would like.

He went to the cake shop and chose one, with lots of delicious cream spread across the top of it. He purchased the cake and was walking back to his aunt's house with a friend, carefully carrying the cake in both hands in front of him.

They walked up the hill and reached the cemetery of St Saviour's church where he made a casual but rude remark about a relative who was recently deceased, and that he didn't used to get on with. At that instant he felt something impede both his ankles and he fell face down into the cake.

After the sudden shock of ending up face down in the cake, he was helped back onto his feet by his friend. They both checked the pavement to see if there was something that could have tripped him up, but there was nothing there.

Rinaldo said that he had "never believed in spooky things", but this had scared him and in future he would not be so dismissive about ghosts.

St Saviour's church, a Grade I listed building dedicated in 1372.

Mount Boone, Dartmouth

The following is a partial transcript of an article printed in the *Dartmouth & South Hams Chronicle* on 7th February 1908.

GHOST HUNTING AT DARTMOUTH.

Have you seen the ghost!

This has been the one absorbing question of the week at Dartmouth. In past years stories have been circulated as to the visitations at periodical intervals of a "ghost" at Mount Boone [...].

During the present week excitement reached a high pitch, and the wildest rumours have been afloat, some asserting that a tall figure had been seen to spring from the hedges, and when members of the gentle sex attempted to make their escape, pursue them closely. [...]

With the object of "laying the ghost," bands of men, youths, and mere lads – the majority armed with sticks – have nightly paraded the neighbourhood [...]

News reached the police that the "ghost" had at last been found, and it was a proud but breathless youth who [...] stated that the "ghost" had been caught near the Cemetery [...]. He also volunteered the startling information that the apparition was "spring-heeled," as it had sprung over the hedge [...].

They duly arrived at the spot indicated by the lad, but if they had hoped to find a wanderer from the spiritual world they must have been sorely disappointed, for instead they discovered a shivering half-scared "commercial" of the road surrounded by a crowd of youths. The terror of the poor wretch was increased four-fold by the appearance of the sergeant and the constable, and to them he pleaded to be allowed to continue his tramp to his next place of abode – the workhouse at Totnes. The crowd of heroic ghost seekers, however, had first to be satisfied, and so a match was struck, the boots of the unfortunate tramp were examined in order to prove that they were not "spring-heeled," [...]. And then the wanderer was allowed to continue his weary tramp, the crowd dispersed, and the night's farce ended.

Dartmouth Castle

A personal account of a vigil on the evening of 12th April 2008, by Ken Taylor

I'd wandered off down a tunnel, without a light, and alone. Standing at the entrance to a pitch black store room deep in the bowels of the castle, I suddenly imagined skeletal hands rushing clawing at my face, and a riot of horror movie terrors engulfed me.

Fear of the dark, of being lost, of falling prey to the madness of nightmare... These and other, less easily named, primal fears rose in shocking waves inside me as the sea pounded those massive stone walls in this cold dead of night.

I really shouldn't have left my companions and gone off alone. Such folly can exact a high price - to lose the fight against monstrous fear, and to be overwhelmed by panic, can leave scars of trauma not easily healed even by the sweet tea and counselling that any decent investigation group can muster. I did indeed pay a forfeit, although I didn't realise it at the time.

It was actually only a brief struggle, mercifully, to pull my thoughts out of free-fall, rein in my imagination, and shut the door firmly on the accumulated frights that subconsciously haunt us all.

By mastering my emotions though, forcing the genie back into the bottle, I lost all sensitivity to my surroundings. Now my chance of meeting a real ghost were even less likely than the sea suddenly finding a chink in the armour of that centuries old masonry.

The vigil had been organised jointly by the Bristol Society for Paranormal Research and Investigation, of which I was a patron, and Torbay Investigators of the Paranormal, with whom I'd met while researching *Dartmouth Ghosts & Mysterie*s.

I really enjoy it when groups join forces and pool resources, sharing their results, advice, and insights. The fact is unless we're careful we can end up looking for and finding evidence that only bolsters our own opinions. All too often the bits that don't fit our theories, the irritating anomalies we brush under the carpet, are actually the breadcrumbs of truth. It's a dreadful irony that this all too human trait bedevils paranormal research, which is explicitly devoted to researching the anomalous. The different approaches that groups take, not only keeps everyone flexible (in 2019 BSPRI has a greater focus on the scientific method than it did at the time of this investigation), but helps everybody achieve a broader perspective on the subject that fascinates us all.

Some members of BSPRI assembling before the investigation, at the modern entrance to Dartmouth Castle.

Sometimes, it's only when we stop looking, that we find an important clue, and the Dartmouth Castle vigil forcibly reminded me of that lesson.

9pm found me in the Guard Room of the Battery, in the company of Caroline, Harri, and Wend - we were one of three similar sized groups from BSPRI, investigating the castle in a rota system (TIP organised themselves separately but carefully, so the teams didn't overlap).

We sat around a wooden table, and I noticed a penny lying on it, so I suggested its use as a trigger object (a carefully positioned item that could become a focus for paranormal activity). Caroline noticed a small circular mark, like the sort of ring left by a hot cup, on the table close to her, and moved the coin into its centre.

In one corner of the room was an empty fireplace with a metal grate, and it attracted considerable interest because it appeared to be the source of a clearly audible but randomly spaced 'click' or 'tap' that recurred perhaps half a dozen times. This was first noticed immediately after somebody mentioned a key question in the whole investigation - whether there were any spirits present that actually wished to make contact with us.

Several equipment bags had been left, before the vigil began, in the corner near the fireplace. I suggested something in them might somehow be causing the clicks, and that if we removed them, we could better pinpoint the source of the sound. Upon agreement, I moved them away. The noise did not recur. Whether this cessation occurred because my incursion into the corner disrupted a spirit manifestation, or because there was simply something mundane gradually settling inside one of the bags, is a moot point.

We noticed the coin in the circle was now displaced by at least 1cm. It may be significant that the direction of motion was away from Caroline's notebook, which was on the table and close by - could an accidental nudge have caused the coin to move? However, it may also be significant that the movement was directly toward the fireplace and source of the mysterious sound - could the momentary distraction of our attention from the coin have allowed a discarnate entity the freedom to move it?

It's so tempting to jump to one conclusion or the other, and the evidence could certainly be argued by either side to support their viewpoint. The whole event was recorded by Wend's handheld video camera, but of course that recorded her direction of interest which, along with the rest of us, followed the potentially supernatural misdirection toward the fireplace.

Although a purely materialistic explanation may currently be in vogue, there is much that the scientific method has yet to explain. There are, for instance, a couple of famous physics experiments that produce mutually contradictory results: in one case the equipment is set up to observe how light behaves as a wave, and in the other as a particle. Both experiments work, and each conclusively shows light behaves in the anticipated way. It would be glib to say each experiment found what it expected to find (which would suggest we live in a very strange and magical universe), but at very least we must accept that somehow reality can actually accommodate seemingly irreconcilable opposites.

Closing our minds to an opposing idea leaves us living in a dream. We now know the nature of light is neither particle nor wave, but is something that transcends those narrow definitions and encompasses them both. The fact that *anything* exists at all, is literally incredible and defies explanation as to how. Yet clearly the coin, the circle on the table, the observers, these written words, and now you the reader, all have existence. We're all a part of this grand mystery, and we each have the chance to solve its puzzle. To be fair though, we're only likely to solve our own part of it.

Explanations have come into fashion, and been superseded time after time, and this process of re-evaluation will continue, but because ideological purges and even wars are routinely conducted between opponent ideas, it's important to get some perspective on this. They are only ideas: we can discuss them without torturing or killing anybody.

Many people who appear to be 'sitting on the fence', unwilling to commit to either side, are not lazily avoiding the dilemma but are actively seeking a higher resolution. Eventually perhaps, we may discover a new piece of common ground beneath an open sky, where a daisy is revealed to have both leaves and flowers.

Back in the dark confines of Dartmouth Castle, isolated teams of focussed individuals were confronting their fears and hopes, and carefully noting and sharing their perceptions. Phenomena reported by the BSPRI teams were collated and published on their website (Britton 2006).

BSPRI's excellent published report runs to well over 4,000 words, so clearly the following summary excludes details such as precise time, exact location, demographics of witnesses and anyone else present, as well as the events leading to and following from the incidents. Of course, it is in the analysis of such detailed data, particularly when a site is investigated repeatedly as this one has been, that subtle patterns may one day be recognised. The archives of such investigating organisations includes photographs, video (including infrared) and audio (including infrasound) recordings, and data logged by a wide range of other environmental monitoring equipment, which contain a wealth of information for future study.

The reported incidents below are grouped roughly in thematic, not strictly chronological order.

Old Tower (Gun Tower)

Unspecified location

- ❖ Impressions - The name Montigue (Penny). Pleasant, safe and comforted (Marina).

Basement

- ❖ Physical - Temperature drop (Claire & Richard). Nauseous (Wend). Tingling across shoulders and down back (Wend). Hair standing on end (Richard). As if hit across the bridge of the nose, eyes watering (Andy).
- ❖ Impressions - Rats and cats (Penny). Someone near the small cannon (Gayle & Richard). Edward Jacobs, burly, bearded, aged about thirty, near the top of the stairs and watching the investigators (Caroline). George, stout man with a metallic taste in his mouth, by the stairs (Penny). Rowing boats involved in smuggling (Claire). Men sitting around a table by the fireplace, with female prostitutes (Jamie). Raggedly dressed man with rotten teeth, beard, boils on face, and stink of faeces (Richard & Claire). Vomiting and bringing up blood (Caroline). Delirious, bleeding from nose (Caroline). Accidental death from either the recoil of a cannon or falling rock (Andy). Dying people receiving their last rites, and an 18th century man with a thin mouth and beaky nose, black hair tied in a ponytail with a black bow, holding a book and clothed in black with a cravat of white lace, white stockings and black shoes with buckles (Penny).

Ground Floor

- ❖ Physical - Tight chest, laboured breathing (Gayle). Pain in right leg below the knee (Claire).

- Impressions - Small cannon on the entrance level was from ship, not an original feature of the tower (Andy). Floor level had been changed (Penny). Area by the window by the fireplace was a separate room (Claire). Depression (Richard). Varicose veins in legs (Richard). Seated man with head in his hands (Wend). Female prostitute (Claire). Brutal man, an outsider and a bully who was feared by other men (Caroline). Friendly fire incident in the 1790s involving Lieutenant John Dryden and Sergeant Bowsman: the last breaths of the dying man who had been accidentally shot in the stomach (Penny). A man approximately 5' 8" (1.73m) tall, clothed in a leather jerkin, holding in his hand the sort of a weapon known as a pike (Penny). Roger Grahame, well-muscled, 5' 8" (1.73m) tall, holding a pike (Richard). Panicked people rushing around in dense smoke with buckets of water to dowse a fire, bell of St Petrox was being rung (Penny).

First Floor

- Physical - Laboured breathing (Phil). Colder in the middle of the room (Harri). Warm, as if there were a lit fire (Caroline). Stomach pains, headache at top of head (Gayle). Cobwebs brushing face (Richard).
- Impressions - Movement, energy racing around (Caroline). Figures of authority: officers wearing tricorn hats (Jamie). The name Hudson and date 1736 (Phil). Two men, one young with dirty, straggling blond hair, the other in his forties; they would play cards, and watch for ships (Phil). Two men, one in his forties, the other younger; dating to the reign of James I - 1603 to 1625 (Penny).

Battlements

- Impressions - A tall ship on fire, out to sea (Penny).

New Tower

Casemate 1

This is the nearest room of the casemate, which is the technical word for a fortified gun emplacement.

- ❖ Heard - Raps on the decking (Penny & Phil). Groan lasting two seconds (Emma, Gayle & Jamie).
- ❖ Smelled - Hay (Claire & Richard).
- ❖ Seen - Light moving vertically down (Gayle). Lights on wall with the cast iron sign: first blue, then green then red (Phil, Penny, and Phil respectively). Movement around the cannon (Claire, Emma, Jamie, & Richard).
- ❖ Impressions - Man, tall and strong, who threatened and beat people and laughed at the way they cowered (Caroline). Gardener surname, 52 (Phil).

Lighting Passage and Stores

- ❖ Physical - something touched hair on head (Wend). Something touched hair on head (Caroline). Something blew on face (Harri).
- ❖ Heard - Shuffling sound encountered at the far, bricked-up end, the sound followed the witness all the way out (Andy).
- ❖ Seen - White light moved across the door to Magazine 2 (Andy). Misty shape in Magazine 2, apparently checking stores: the figure seemed short and fat, with small circular spectacles (Penny).
- ❖ Impressions - Followed by a presence on way out of the passage (Wend).

Casemate 2

The two furthermost rooms of the casemate.

- Physical - Headache (Gayle). Nauseous (Penny).
- Heard - A squeaky laugh (Ken & Wend).
- Smelled - Smoke of a fire (Claire).
- Seen - Misty light (Claire). Flash of light (Gayle). Spherical white light (Andy). Two flashes of white light (Emma). Lights and movement (Jamie).
- Impressions - Vermin, including rats (Richard). Cat in the corner by the door to Casemate 1 (Claire). French people (Claire). Someone was ambushed and their throat slit (Penny). Thomas (Penny). Looking through someone else's eyes, feeling the investigators were interfering and shouldn't be there (Jamie). William - Bill or Billy - Jarvis (Andy). Men sweating doing drills, high adrenaline, keen to avoid mistakes (Claire & Richard).

Guard Room

Recorded - Infrasound at 15hz.

- Physical - Cobwebs on face, and spectacles on nose (Claire). Hair on head touched, and cobwebs on face (Richard).
- Seen - Wriggling light (Richard). Red light by the fireplace (Caroline).
- Heard - Tapping (see above, re trigger object).
- Impressions - William or James, a boy of five or six years, with long hair and dressed scruffily (Caroline).

Guardians from the Past, Strete Gate

In 2002 a young married couple were camping overnight on the beach at Strete Gate, enjoying a romantic evening under a sky enlivened with a meteor shower, when things took an unexpected turn. The wife, Anna, tells the tale.

"Suddenly I get yelled at by five gentlemen in green uniform. At first I thought 'Have we done something wrong?' It's not a military area any more so I was puzzled as to why they were holding guns at the time, because at first I mistook them for police officers and thought we were about to be told to go home and pack up or something along those lines.

"It took me a moment or two to work out that these men were not police officers and my husband could not see or hear them! But they still continued to yell at me telling me it was unsafe to be there, that we had to leave now or we could get badly hurt or even killed, and they were VERY insistent and kept saying we needed to leave now or we could end up like them. I had by this time worked out they were ghosts given as my husband could not see or hear them and their insistence actually prompted me to tell my husband that we needed to go home and it had to be now!

"In the morning I heard on the local radio news that the bomb squad were called in to the Street Gate area of the beach. A dog walker had found a WW2 shell that had washed up with the high tide on the beach that night, right where myself and my husband had been camped!

Those uniforms were not modern day army uniforms. I have since come to believe that they approached me that night to move us away from danger they knew was coming."

Coastguard Cottages, Dartmouth

This is an account of a story told to Ken Taylor shortly after his book *Dartmouth Ghosts & Mysteries* was released in 2006. It is a very interesting story and Ken is glad it can be included in this volume.

The Coastguard Cottages, Castle Road, consist of eight cottages. At the west end is the large Watch House where the principle officer would have lived, and at the east end is the Lookout, now a two-storey house (originally a single storey). The Coastguard built the complex in 1902 and it is thought they were vacated some time after the Second World War. They were rented out in the mid-1960s and John Sansom bought them in 1972.

On 29th August 2006 Ken was contacted by John Clarke who had been living at No. 2 Coastguard cottages. John recalled that a lady called Mary Burnett, wife of an Indian army colonel, who lived at No. 7 had been terrified of entering the Watch House.

She had been told that the ghost of an English airman, a pilot, haunted the Watch House and that his ghost was still there. Mary's cottage was too small for a freezer in those days, which was around the mid-1970s. She had permission from the owner of the Watch House, who was seldom there, to use his freezer. This was very kind of the owner but Mary was too afraid to go into the Watch house alone. She preferred someone to go in with her, which would sometimes be John's children when they came to stay. Initially the children only visited as theirs was a holiday home. Unfortunately, Mary and her husband are now deceased.

Another incident retold to Ken was something which John's wife Ann, now deceased, had witnessed in the mid-1990s. It was during the daytime when Ann "saw a small child, a young girl, walk thought one wall, walk across the downstairs front room and through the other wall." This means that Ann was in cottage No. 2 and saw the child walk through the wall from the first cottage, No. 1, though her front room, and disappear through the wall into cottage No. 3.

John recalls that she had "no doubt whatsoever" about what she had seen and yet "was not frightened by it." John added that he was once told "that a little girl had fallen down the stairs of one of the cottages and died."

Although this could perhaps account for the ghostly sighting of the child, there does not appear any evidence at this time for it.

John Sansom also had a story which had been told to him. "The story was of a man who'd died in one of the cottages, something like No. 3 or 4, I think. He was a holidaymaker staying there after they had been sold and used as holiday cottages. He had loved going back year after year. He was reputed to be seen standing in a corner with a bucket and spade and a crabbing net."

John Sansom said he thinks that this is probably highly unlikely, and he is not a believer in such tales himself. "Much in this field is speculation" he said, and then added "but I suppose patterns might emerge which substantiates or help establish the validity of one story as opposed to another."

Ghostly Activity in Archway Drive, Dartmouth

In 2006 a Dartmouth couple were so troubled by paranormal activity at their home in Archway Drive that they considered asking a priest to conduct an exorcism. Instead, they contacted the *Dartmouth Chronicle* in a plea for an explanation - and an article was published in July (Anon 2006).

The couple, Dawn and Michael Yates, had lived in their home for six years: two years had gone by without odd happenings, then occasional incidents occurred, but in the last two years activity became increasingly frequent. Even their daughter, who was just ten months old, seemed able to sense when the alleged ghost was manifesting.

Dawn told the Chronicle reporter about electric lights switching off without known cause, and doors would open and close without reason - even their bathroom door which took some effort to move at all due to the thick carpet beneath it.

Dawn said she didn't feel the ghost meant them any harm, but clearly the family wanted peace to return to their home. In the article she asked for anyone to contact them if they knew anything relevant about the history of their house.

When Ken Taylor was at the Harbour Bookshop, signing books for the launch of his *Dartmouth Ghosts & Mysteries* on 31st October 2006, Dawn took the opportunity to approach him about her case.

Happily, she said that things had been much quieter in the past months. They had hung a rosary in the house, which seemed to help. She added that after a period of normality she had taken it down but inexplicable events had started to happen again, so she put it back up, and their home promptly became calm again.

The Old Ambulance HQ, Dartmouth

The following tale was given to me by Nicholas Davies, who was a member of Dartmouth St John Ambulance between 1991 and 2012, based at the old Headquarters on College Way.

"I had been a member of the Dartmouth Division since I was a Cadet in 1991 and almost from the outset I had heard the stories of the building being haunted. I have always prided myself on being open minded but admittedly I had to draw the line somewhere, and although many had laid claim to an "Encounter" over the years, I dismissed it all as gossip and local folklore based on the area's long past. In short I didn't believe in ghosts!

"The Headquarters was built on reclaimed land which was originally the site of a boatyard. Local legend had it that a man committed suicide in that yard by hanging himself from the rafters and his spirit still haunted the site.

"The boatyard was demolished in the Second World War to make way for public air raid shelters, these in turn were partially demolished and converted into the Headquarters for the Dartmouth Ambulance and St John Ambulance Brigade in 1958. In the 1980s the Dartmouth Ambulance station moved up to new premises half way up the hill opposite BRNC, and St John Ambulance remained in the building. This building in turn has now been demolished to make way for luxury flats.

"Many people reported encounters with the restless spirit of the man who killed himself. I never believed any of it. In the summer of 1996 my inner sceptic got a very rude wake-up call!

"By then I had moved up into the Brigade, and established myself well into the Division. As well as assisting with running the Cadets and being the Brigade rep on the Committee, I had been assigned the role of Divisional Storekeeper and as such had the privilege of being one of the few lay members with keys to the building. It was on one such visit to the Headquarters the encounter happened.

"I was gathering the supplies needed for a large joint cover event with two neighbouring divisions of Totnes and Brixham, taking them from the lower storeroom and assembling them in the main hall ready for collection on the following weekend. It was a hot summer day, and the weather made me leave the main door of the HQ open which led out onto the main road. That was something I didn't normally do when working in the building alone.

"The Building was on two levels connected by a small stairwell. The hall and garage with main door and foyer were on the upper floor, whilst the kitchen, office, toilets and stores were all on the lower level.

"I was in the office on the lower floor, sat at the office desk checking the paperwork, when I heard the main door slam shut with an enormous bang which made me jump feet! After gathering myself, I called up to see who it was. I got no answer. I called again, and again I got silence. Just after I called the second time I heard the STOMP STOMP STOMP of slow moving heavy booted feet walking across the hall and stopping in the centre of the room.

"Figuring it was my Superintendent calling in during his work break I got up to investigate. I called him by name as I left the office asking him what was up, but again no answer. I got to the top of the steps and discovered the main door was still open and exactly as I had left it although I did hear it slam shut loudly, as I expect everyone else in the area did. I took a quick look outside - no one in sight nor any car I recognised parked opposite, which struck me as peculiar, and I continued into the hall.

"No one was in the hall. It was completely deserted. What was more, there was no indication anybody had ever entered, nothing had moved and nothing was out of place. I must point out at this point that the floor of the hall was polished wood and the hall floor echoed throughout the building - nobody could have entered or exited the premises without being heard.

"I continued down into the kitchen and even the toilets. Not a soul was in sight. As I checked the hall the temperature dropped suddenly and noticeably as I approached the centre of the hall despite the hot day, and it sent shivers down my spine! Something made me look up and I discovered with a shudder I was actually standing right under one of the metal roof rafters that's when the realisation hit me I'd had my own encounter!

"It did leave me shaken, and I didn't speak of it for a long time after. I didn't run screaming from the building or anything dramatic but carried on rather nervously doing what I went down for. It scared me yes, but I had a job to do and I had to get it done. Although my mind was preoccupied for a long time trying to find some logical explanation for my experience, all of my theories and own investigations came to nothing. There was no earthly explanation for my encounter and I had to accept it for what it was, my first brush with the paranormal.

"I never had another encounter within the building although my perspective changed dramatically thereafter and I never looked at the Headquarters in the same way again. I developed a new respect for it, an awareness that something was present in the building and although not everyone had an experience, it made its presence felt to me and in a strange way that made me feel a little special. My open mindedness had had its horizons broadened just a little more which, I feel looking back, was no bad thing."

2nd point of view

The following story was sent to me by David Drury who recalls events from even earlier times.

"The ambulance crews, myself included, always thought the building was haunted. In the mid-seventies I was stationed at Dartmouth Ambulance station and strange things, such as banging of doors, footsteps walking across the wooden floor, things being thrown down the stairs, and doors opening were sometimes heard.

"We would always call out to the sounds but when we went to see who was there, the room was empty. When I left the service I still used the room as I am a member of the St John Ambulance. We used to hold first aid courses in the main room where all the activity used to occur. On several occasions people would complain of feeling icy cold even when they were sat below a gas heater. When we moved them to another seat they would stop feeling cold.

"We came to the conclusion that the steps we hear were the last steps of the former resident before they hanged themselves."

A Chilling Experience at Alma Place, Kingswear

The following account was originally sent to Ken Taylor (editor of this book) from Peter Watts on 1st October 2008. It relates to a time some 50 years ago when Peter and his wife, May, were living at Alma Place, Kingswear. He recalls vividly the experience he had whilst living there.

The very first evening that he commenced work on the lower staircase he agreed to 'babysit' whilst May went up the road to spend a couple of hours with her sister, giving her a well-deserved break in her daily routine. Peter decided to work harder and, with luck, finish painting and hopefully repaper the walls the next evening. All was going well, the children were fast asleep and he was comforted in the knowledge that May was able to enjoy a few hours respite.

The staircase was of such design that after ascending ten steps or so, it took a sharp right turn to the first landing. At the turn of the stairs was a most unusual alcove, of such dimension that it could easily have secreted a small person.

Peter had often noticed it but could never comprehend the reason for its construction in that particular place. As the house was at least one hundred years old, it may have simply been left when possible reconstruction had taken place at some time in the past and so it was left as it was.

Peter said "Late in the evening I was in the act of removing some of the wallpaper in the subject area when I experienced a most unusual feeling... The atmosphere took on a distinct chill and for the first time in my life I could literally feel the hair rise on the back of my neck. I told myself that I was imagining things, that maybe I had been working too hard (or something) and decided to cease work for a while and make a cup of tea.

"About fifteen minutes later I returned to the scene, commenced stripping more paper from within the alcove... The same atmosphere returned, a distinct feeling of a presence of some kind. The whole experience became so intense that I decided to move up the stairs to the landing and start painting the balustrade.

"No matter how hard I tried I was unable to shake off the feeling that I was in the presence of another being. The chill in the air was still apparent, I simply had to stop work altogether and call it a day. My wife came home about an hour afterwards. I chose not to tell her about it and put it down to a figment of my imagination. In any event, May was alone in the house all day and I had no wish to frighten her."

The next evening, after finishing his meal Peter settled down to work again. May was home this evening and was sitting downstairs sewing. He decided to continue painting the balustrade, stay away from the alcove area and had a small radio with him playing at a low volume so as not to disturb the sleeping children.

He recalls "Within minutes the feeling of a 'presence' returned. I decided that the only thing I could do was try and deny the unusual situation and work as quickly as possible to get away from the area. It took me two more evenings... my work suffered, it was certainly sub-standard but for the whole of the time I worked in that area, most especially near the alcove I felt I was in the presence of another being. To be quite honest I was really scared! I continued working on the next staircase leading to the attic rooms without incident, but, whenever I passed the alcove area on the lower stairs I felt as though I was in the presence of another being... *That I was being watched!*"

Some time later Peter and his wife moved to New Zealand and after spending twenty years there they relocated to Queensland, Australia and moved close to friends, one of whom had lived at Alma Place when she was young.

One night as they were reminiscing about old times she told Peter that as a child she had slept in a room right next to that little alcove on the stairs and that she had experienced the same feeling as he described for the whole time that she lived there. Every time she went to bed or came down the stairs and had to go past that area, she used to run.

Peter's wife May had been listening quietly to all this and then said that one of the reasons she was glad to leave Alma Place was for precisely the same reasons. She said that she had never mentioned it to Peter as she felt too embarrassed to do so!

Disturbance at The Royal Castle Hotel, Dartmouth

The Royal Castle Hotel, Dartmouth has had some very famous guests in the past. Queen Victoria was a guest there, also Cary Grant and Agatha Christie. Built in 1639, the facade is of Georgian style and a fine example of an English coaching house. It is reputedly haunted and even has a phantom stagecoach which at the dead of night has been heard to draw up at the front door.

Colin Drury, a resident from Dartmouth remembers an incident which happened back in the 1990s when he was contacted by the hotel and asked if he could decorate some of the bedrooms.

He was given a three-day turnover to decorate a room and then he was to begin on another. On the morning he began work he called at reception to find out which room he was to start on. He was directed to start in a particular room, which Colin referred to as the King's room, because it was unoccupied.

Assuming that it was unlocked he got half way up the staircase when he could hear shouting and what sounded like an argument coming from that room. He said the shouting was very loud and it sounded like things were being thrown about. Outside the room there was broken glass and a nail brush lying on the carpet.

Thinking there was still someone staying in the room and that a mistake had been made, he quickly went back down to the reception to check. The receptionist said he must be mistaken because there wasn't anyone staying in that room. It had been kept empty so he could work on it. The receptionist went to where the keys were hung up and, sure enough, the key was still there.

They checked with the housekeeper who had the master-key for the room and then they went back up the stairs to try and find out what or who was in there. On arriving at the door they found that it was locked and that the room was totally silent. They looked at one another and apprehensively they slowly opened the door.

The room was in total disarray. There was soap on the floor, things had been moved about and the drapes which had hung around the four- poster bed had been pulled down. The room was wrecked, but there was nobody in there.

Who or what caused the damage to the room is a mystery. Such a lot of disturbance in the room, both noise and physical upheaval, might possibly point to poltergeist activity. What stirred up this type of activity is unknown, but to move things and break things in that way suggests a lot of energy was needed.

Colin didn't hear or see anything else untoward whilst he was decorating the room, but it did make him feel a little uneasy.

The Highwayman

The Royal Castle Hotel has served the community of Dartmouth in many different ways over the years. In the early 1950s it was used for Christmas parties for children who had lost a parent or parents. Daphne May Stockton was six years old at the time and had been invited to attend the party as she also had lost a parent.

She recollects that they had to leave their coats in the room next door. "We saw something in that room. It was very cold in there and when we asked why, we were told it was the ghost of the Highwayman. From that day to now I believe it is haunted."

The Mantle of Cornu, a Blackawton Tale

In the south of the picturesque village of Blackawton lies an old lane that runs due east off Vicarage Road, toward a stream that flows south eventually to join The Gara which empties into the sea at Strete Gate. This lane has an unusual local reputation - mostly it is tranquil and known as something of a lover's lane, but sometimes people sense they are being followed by someone whose intentions are far from peaceful. It is also the setting for a strange ghost story told by a woman who does not wish to be identified.

"Both myself and my partner attended a bonfire night after work only to see a circle of hooded robed individuals around the fire. They were in a formation and I could tell these ghosts were the real witches of Blackawton, and they were not happy about something. My partner could also see them and he was a little puzzled as to why others were not interacting with them, I had to explain to him that their closed minds mean they cannot see them or they refuse to see them. We decided to stay when everyone else had drifted home after the fireworks. I wanted to see what these people were doing, but they just seemed to vanish.

"My partner told me he was approached by one of them, a man wearing a wooden mask who said his name was Marcus, and the spectre asked him to 'take up the mantle of Cornu.' My partner wasn't sure what was meant but I'm sure it's the same Marcus I had met in the churchyard of St Michael's, in Blackawton...

"From the time I started pre-school at around four years old, right up until I was about ten, I was friends with the ghost of a little girl who calls herself Emily. This little girl (among others) looms around the churchyard and school area. I don't know if she was a 'native' of the Blackawton area or if she's a traveller of the ley-line, and stuck at the church.

"She died of an illness either in St Michael's tower or another church tower along the ley line. This line has been traced all the way up to Dartmoor and all the way out to sea – just follow the names of places starting with the name 'Black' such as Blackpool Sands, Blackawton, and Blackdown etc. Blackawton seems to be a nexus point of this ley-line, and the Iron Age fort at Blackdown Rings is another.

"This little ghost was one of the reasons I used to get bullied in a Church of England primary school because I would be seen talking to the air at the old school gates that lead to the school from the churchyard (when I was ten years old I managed to shut down part my 'gift' due to the fear of the bullying). The one thing I always noticed with her she always looks sickly and sad in a lonely kind of way. She's the child of an accused witch of Blackawton, and the anger of her father's spirit still lashes out from time to time if you go around the graveyard of the church.

"Her father was accused of witchcraft and executed for it, and although his spirit seems calm he wants his story to be known – that he was innocent and didn't bring harm to people as they had claimed. He calls himself Marcus but I cannot find any record of him, at least not in Blackawton.

"The main report of these ghosts is a feeling of uneasiness when walking past the graveyard or through it both in the day and night, worse at night."

Tragedy at the Britannia Royal Naval College, Dartmouth

Tragedy struck on the morning of 18th September 1942 when the Britannia Royal Naval College was bombed during an air-raid causing extensive damage to part of the building. Petty Officer Ellen Whittall who was a telegraphist at the college had just entered the ladies' rest-room when the building was hit. Fortunately, much of the rest of the building was deserted at the time due to it being summer break.

Known as Nella to family and friends, Ellen Victoria Foulkes was born in 1901 at Birmingham, and married Frederick Whittall at Stratford-upon-Avon in 1923. She was widowed in 1934. Ellen was a member of the Women's Royal Naval Service, popularly known as the Wrens.

There have been various reports of unusual happenings around the area of the rest-room and the corridor outside it, including sudden drops in temperature for no apparent reason.

A cadet who took a photograph of the corridor, for a keepsake, having had his photographs developed saw what appeared to be a figure standing there, outside the rest-room. He was certain that when he took the photograph the corridor had been empty, there was nobody else there.

Ellen was buried in Efford Cemetery, Plymouth, the only fatality at the college during WW2. In 2005 a memorial plaque in her honour was unveiled at the college by Prince Michael of Kent, it is situated on the wall outside the rest-room where she was killed.

Eye-witness accounts of the bombing raid can be found online (Two Jays, 2019), and I'm grateful to Ken Taylor for uncovering the biographical details of her life.

Eight Short Stories

The Grove, Blackawton

The witness who elsewhere describes the incident of four glasses breaking at The George Inn, further informs us that the public house isn't the only spot in Blackawton to have a long-standing tradition of poltergeist activity.

People have spoken of houses near the entrance of The Grove where small items such as towels or toys have been thrown around. The culprit is rarely seen but has been described as looking like an old monk, one young witness (whose parents assumed he was an 'imaginary friend') referred to him by the French name Jacques.

His mischievous antics however may belie a more benign nature as the mother of a baby son who was poorly, awoke in the night to see a figure standing over his cot. She naturally assumed it was her husband standing there, but when she rolled over she saw he was still lying beside her. That night her child slept peacefully, and in due course recovered.

The Keep, Dartmouth

The Keep is situated in the Mount Boone area of Dartmouth. It's a Grade II listed building with views over to the mouth of the Dart estuary. It was built in or around 1850 to resemble a medieval castle surrounded many years ago by beautiful gardens.

This is an account of a story told to me by someone who has lived in Dartmouth for many years. There is a lane which now divides the gardens which belonged to The Keep. Many years ago there was a bridge which went above and over the lane, which at some point in time was either destroyed or taken down.

A man who was walking down the lane one night happened to look up and saw something ghostly in appearance, walking above the lane, where the bridge would once have been.

Oldstone Mansion, Blackawton

In the autumn of 1984 a couple with a child of around two-and-a-half years were driving from Blackawton to Dartmouth. As they slowly passed the ruins of Oldstone Mansion the young girl, Anna, started demanding they should stop so she could go and play with two children she saw playing there.

That struck the couple as unusual as their daughter was actually a rather shy child, and they looked to see if they recognised either of the children, but there was no one to be seen.

Anna kept insisting they stop, pleading with her parents that she could save the children from a fire.

It wasn't until later that the mother discovered that the building had indeed been gutted by fire - in 1895 - but there were no reports of fatalities in the blaze.

Is it possible the little girl had somehow succeeded in protecting the two children she alone could see?

Bayards Cove Inn, Dartmouth

Originally a merchant's house, and formerly known as Agincourt House, this well-known building in Lower Street has stone walls dating to the 14th century and is regarded as one of the oldest houses in Dartmouth (second only to the Cherub Inn, in Higher Street). Bayards Cove Inn is shown on the back cover of this book. In most centuries since then it has been subject to waves of modernisation and remodelling.

Thelma Jenkins worked at the Agincourt in the late 1990s when she heard a strange story...

Long ago a merchant's daughter had drowned and her body was laid to rest in one of the rooms which, when Thelma worked there, was used as a bedroom. It was said that the top of the wardrobe in that room would always be wet for no reason.

Dartmouth Hospital

This story was given to me by a nurse who had been working at Dartmouth Hospital. She recalled that whilst she was working there she saw a figure which was on the other side of some frosted glass. It was walking up the corridor and then went down the stairs. She quickly checked to see if she could see who it was, but there was nobody there and she could not hear a sound.

Later, whilst talking to other staff members she told them what she had seen. They said it was the ghost of someone who once lived in a flat above the hospital.

Other members of staff said that they sometimes heard footsteps when they were in the staff room, but when they checked there was never anybody there.

St Saviour's Church, Dartmouth

A holidaymaker returning to Hungary had a shock when she was looking over some photos that she took in Dartmouth while visiting her son Tamas. Szabo Drimusch hadn't seen her son for two years and they'd both been very excited about her visit.

Tamas decided to show his mother some of the local churches. Naturally, their tour included the 14th century church of St Saviour, Anzac Street, where she took some photographs.

After returning home to Hungary, Szabo was shocked when she looked at one of Tamas standing in the centre aisle of the church. She contacted him and told him that there was something strange in the photo with him. It looked like a ghost!

Tamas said that they hadn't noticed anything unusual at the time, but when they looked at the photo there was clearly 'something' there that that couldn't explain.

The vicar of St Saviour's, Will Hazlewood, commented on the story, saying he'd not heard of any unexplained appearances at the church, and that it was all a bit of a mystery (Hunter, 2016).

The Moving Gravestone, Strete

I was told this charming little tale by Kath Bardon. She remembers that when she was at primary school she was told a very strange story about a grave in the graveyard of St Michael's at Strete.

It was rumoured that the person who was buried in the grave had wanted to be buried inside the church, but was buried outside in the graveyard instead.

The children said that the gravestone moved a bit closer to the church every year.

Woman in White, Dartmouth

The following is a transcript of an anonymous article printed in the *Dartmouth & South Hams Chronicle* on 09 August 1872.

The Rev. W. Stenner, Independent minister, Dartmouth, about thirty years ago, on returning home from a pastoral visit late at night, on turning a corner of one of the narrow streets of this very ancient town, saw, to his great astonishment, a short distance from him, a tall figure in white. Could it be a ghost? And did he really behold one? Well, he would see. On the figure went with noiseless tread, and at a distance Mr Stenner followed, until it, suddenly, as it was, vanished through a door. The next morning Mr Stenner called at the house at the door of which he saw the figure vanish. The result of the visit was, one of the ladies of the house was known occasionally to "walk in her sleep", and from sundry signs it was evident it was this lady that Mr Stenner saw and followed up the previous night. She had risen from her bed, opened the front door of the house, perambulated the streets, and returned again to her house and bed unknown to her friends. Had the vision been seen by persons of less presence of mind, a very pretty ghost story might have been the result. From the *Leisure Hour*, Aug. 1872.

The George, Blackawton

There are plenty of haunted pubs in Britain, but The George Inn has had perhaps more than its fair share of poltergeist activity. The George is located deep in the Devon countryside between Dartmouth and Totnes, in the little village of Blackawton.

This small community, six miles west of Dartmouth, is famed for its annual worm charming competition which celebrates the arcane art of gathering earthworms without digging. The village was evacuated on 20th December 1943, during the Second World War so that American Forces could practise for D-Day landings; and later in that war it received evacuees.

The George Inn, Blackawton.

A psychic investigation at this well-known haunted pub suggests that an angry mob once killed an innocent man and that the murder has gone unrecognised since the eighteenth century.

Tracey Clark, a former landlady at The George Inn worked as a nurse in a local hospital and during a particularly long night shift she told the author about the almost daily ghostly events.

Tracey and Bob Clark took over the running of the pub in June 2007 and the family experienced a catalogue of paranormal phenomena including poltergeist activity and the presence of at least six ghosts.

The ground floor manifested several female spirits: one with arms open to welcome you, but another, Tracey explained "was a stunningly beautiful woman with a very nasty streak. She was vindictive and we think that she was connected with the murder."

Drawing of mysterious shadowy figure seen by Curtis.

The stairs and landing were haunted by five year-old William, who had long blond hair. His footsteps were often heard, and he rattled door handles and opened doors on the first floor. Tracey and Bob's son Curtis drew a picture after a small figure ran through his room which overlooks the front of the building.

William may also have been responsible for other pranks. Tracey recalled "The cold tap in the bathroom sometimes turns itself on. One evening in September I noticed the tap was running, a steady stream, so I said out loud, 'Can you turn that off please?' And it stopped as I looked at it. The tap didn't physically turn but it stopped, really weird!" Tracey also reported seeing the bathroom door slowly open. "Something opened that door!"

Perhaps William was also responsible for the poltergeist phenomena that began in April 2007. Tracey recalled "Pennies and two-pence pieces would appear in the shower. I was thinking 'have I dropped it there?' But why would I have money on me in the shower? You usually don't have anything on you when you go in the shower! The first time it happened I thought nothing of it. It has happened half a dozen times since then."

The TV remote control went missing for two days and according to Tracey there was no way that it could have been hidden anywhere. By the third night she was really fed up and thought about getting "one of those multi-functional jobs." In bed that night as she pulled back the blanket she saw the remote control was there - it was even facing towards the TV. She had made the bed that morning herself, and it wasn't there then.

That was also the night the banging on her bedroom door began. This was in early June, and her sleep became so badly disturbed that when she heard about the Hidden Realms Paranormal Investigators, she wanted them to investigate.

An initial investigation

Members of the Hidden Realms team spent several hours in various parts of the building.

Mike Harbidge, investigator and the group's webmaster commented "The George Inn was a very interesting place to spend the night. Because of its long, colourful history we were all hoping for a fruitful investigation, which indeed we got. We are open-minded and use traditional methods (such as dowsing and mediumship) alongside the equipment, experiments and methods that come with the scientific aspect of investigating the paranormal." Equipment used during the vigil included a beam-break motion detector, a locked-off video camera, and a digital audio recorder.

The night was unusually quiet in terms of poltergeist activity, but the sensitives picked up on some points of interest. While one of them was sitting in the upstairs lounge, she began to 'link-in' to the energy of a male who was wearing a type of flat cap, a shirt with rolled up sleeves and a waistcoat.

She said "He kept referring to me as 'Missy'. He spoke in a strong Devonshire accent which was quite difficult to understand. I asked for his name and in response got the name Bert."

She also felt that he'd lived there for a long time with his wife, but when he was asked if they'd had children, he seemed to get very agitated. At that point, Pete (another of the group's sensitives) entered the room. The male energy Bert appeared to say "Why him be here Missy?"

The spirit then became silent.

Ghostly monks have been seen in and around The George Inn since the 1960s at least. Curtis, Tracey's son, saw a figure wearing a cloak and cowl, possibly one of the monks that have been seen at the Inn on previous occasions. Tracey herself saw three monks come through the wall in the same room. "They were very humble and peaceful, they were just passing through doing their own thing, bless them. I've only seen them once, and that was in the middle of the day."

The monk, drawn by Curtis.

During an investigative session members of the Hidden Realms team used a planchette - a small piece of wood with a hole for a pencil - which was placed on a piece of paper on a table. The investigators sat in a circle around the table and lightly laid one finger each on it. They invited the spirit to use the team's energy to move it, to write or draw something.

A monk appeared to make contact, and he responded to

questions, saying that he worked on the land and he signed his name simply with an X.

But the biggest mystery surrounds the lynching, which is thought to date to 1747. Kim, one of the group's sensitives, said the man was called George Baker (or Barker) and he had longish dark hair, and was aged around forty. His lover - Abigail - had been falsely accused of a crime, apparently by Josey, the beautiful yet flawed woman who was haunting the bar.

George Baker was running to Abigail's defence, desperately trying to reach the Inn to halt the trial, which was being conducted in an upstairs room, but he was stopped by the mob. They attacked him with knives and pitchforks in the field at the rear of the Inn.

Kim described the scene: "The man is half lying on the ground at the edge of the field, he is propped up on one elbow holding out his arm, as though beseeching, begging to someone at the Inn to help him. He is distressed, sorry, frightened. The mob murdered him right there at the edge of the field. They buried his body in an unmarked grave in unhallowed ground, and innocent Abigail was taken away and hanged.

"They said that the woman (Abigail) killed a person (not sure if a man or child but it was definitely male), they said she poisoned him. But she did not kill him, she helped to make people better, helped deliver babies, nursed people, but they are blaming her for his death. He was ill."

At that point Kim became unsure if the female was called Abigail or Hannah. The sensitives in the group became aware of the presence of a man clothed in black thought to be a pastor, who was wearing a domed hat with a broad, flat, circular rim. It was felt that he was instrumental in persecuting Abigail (Hannah).

With so much activity going on, and pieces of the jigsaw beginning to fit together, Tracey said she felt that "something happened here and they (the spirits) want us to find out what it is. We're being led to look into it."

Research into the history of the building has failed to confirm or refute the romantic yet tragic tale.

The second investigation

The paranormal activity continued, and on one Sunday a wide range of unsettling phenomena was experienced...

- Bob and Tracey were startled by the fire alarm 8.30am (no fault was found on the mains powered alarm, and no physical cause was established).
- Curtis repeatedly saw the ghostly figure of 'the lady in black' - Josey - wandering around downstairs.
- Tracey glimpsed a phantom dog in the main bar, and smelled it too.
- Small items were found to have mysteriously moved around in the couple's dressing room, on the first floor. All this activity happened in just one day at this highly haunted Inn.

With so much activity continuing at the Inn it was decided that Hidden Realms should return for a further investigation.

As part of their investigation, Hidden Realms set up a digital voice recorder (Olympus VN2100PC) in the downstairs passage between the two bars where the spirit called Josey had been seen to walk. The recorder was switched on after the Inn closed, and when everyone was going to bed. It was left to record all night (on standard quality).

When they played it back the team heard a number of bangs, taps and scraping noises that defy immediate explanation. There was also what sounded like a male voice pleading for "Help."

An equally dramatic mood-change occurred in the first floor dressing room where one of the sensitives became aware of a woman floating above them near the ceiling of the room: "She was face down with arms and legs splayed out. Her dark eyes were wide open in a face framed with jet black hair. She looked quite young. I asked her name and was given the name Dorian (I am not sure if this was her name or a name associated with her). I was also given the image of a letter and a carriage and that she had committed suicide by drowning."

Betty, another sensitive, saw a purple cloud enveloping the whole group, protecting them.

The sensitives asked the lady to step down into the circle. It was initially thought that the female spirit was residual energy but this would be proven wrong. Residual energy is like a replay of events that have already happened - there is no communication or interaction between the witness and the phenomena, which is simply something seen, heard or smelt (as in perfume or tobacco).

The woman's spirit descended from the ceiling and entered the circle. Dennis, another member of the team, described it saying "This was followed by the most dramatic temperature drop any of us had ever experienced, completely taking our breath away. It was like being immersed in freezing water full of ice blocks. Sounds dramatic? It was! It took quite a while for us to recover."

Another sensitive described how "Everyone pulled back at the icy dampness that surrounded her. It was like having an icy cold shower. We were all shivering at this point and it was quite uncomfortable. She seemed to envelop the whole inner area of the circle and her shape was dynamic, her dress and hair floating as if still in water.

"She was looking about her and I had a feeling of terrible loneliness and loss. I was so cold it was difficult to speak, but I asked if she could see a bright light. At this point I saw the image of a light above her which almost looked like a beautiful full moon. She appeared to be looking up at the light and I asked if she would like to go to the light.

"I explained about the light and told her that we could help her if this is what she wanted.

"She then seemed to rise from the ground slightly and become smaller and at the same time the light merged with her and they became one and disappeared. When this happened we all began to feel warmer and the atmosphere of the room changed. We felt as though she had entered the light and we said a prayer of thanks."

Kim, one of the sensitives who was also part of the circle commented "It was as though someone had flicked a switch - the atmosphere completely changed, not only did warmth return quickly but a strong sense of peace you could feel all around, I felt very tearful at the end, but happy tears."

It may be significant that the dressing room where that occurred has a slightly slanting floor. Could the sensations of floating in water be caused by the vestibular system (located in the inner ear, which assists with our sense of balance) drifting out of phase with the rest of the body?

This room had also been the main focus for poltergeist activity in recent months. It has en-suite facilities, and phenomena ranged from coins appearing in the shower, to taps turning on and off. On another occasion a loud bang was heard and a huge conch shell which had been displayed on the back of the cistern had fallen into the toilet. If the cat hadn't been sat on Tracey's lap the animal would have got the blame. The rim of the toilet was broken but the shell - which was much more delicate - was still intact. Such events appear wholly independent of an effect on anybody's physical balance or lack thereof.

Was the drowned woman responsible for the poltergeist activity? The shower, taps and toilet all have clear connections with water. And, if so, assuming the woman had now finally found peace by entering 'the light', would these paranormal phenomena cease?

Psychometry

The very next night, Tracey wrote in her diary "Very cold in the dressing room this evening. The tap came on quite fully, I asked out loud for it to go off and it did! An almost exact replay of previous events."

Tracey also recalled that a 5p coin appeared in the shower cubicle. This coin may have a special significance because previously only 1p and 2p coins had appeared – 'copper' coins. Could this new 'silver' coin be a reference to the bright circle of the full moon which was described in the spirit rescue? That vigil, incidentally, was held just three nights after the moon was full.

It was some nights later, a Wednesday night around 10pm, when Curtis went to close the door at the foot of the stairs (which lead up to the family's living rooms). "As he did so," said Tracey "he noticed a 2p coin bouncing down the stairs towards him! It came all the way down and landed in the bar. No one was upstairs at the time, not even the cat."

This coin was collected by a member of Hidden Realms and taken for psychometry readings kindly provided by several very experienced mediums. Psychometry is the apparent psychic ability to sense energy infusing an item, and to discern the object's history by reading that energy (for instance a favourite piece of jewellery could reveal something about the person to whom it belonged).

The three mediums were each presented with the coin in a different location, they hadn't been in contact with each other regarding the coin, and were not told anything about it beforehand.

- ❖ Tony Stockwell (author, psychic medium and television personality) felt that there was a lot of energy attached to the coin. He sensed the spirit of a young woman with dark hair who had an attachment to the Inn in some way. The coin had been sent by spirit as a means of communication, and the energy from the coin made his hand and arm tingle quite strongly - he was surprised at the amount of energy generated by the coin.
- ❖ Ann Benney (well-known medium in the Torbay area) said "Have you got this off a woman? I can sense a feminine energy. Something unpleasant happened to her. There is also a male energy, not immediately connected. I feel a dark swirling, like a 'pool of oil'. I have also got the name 'William' who could have been a horse handler. There is a nearby farm connected with this tragedy."
- ❖ Reverend Denice Vandenburg (Brixham and Paignton Spiritualist Church) said "This coin came bouncing down the stairs – it is an apport. I feel that this may mean a new direction for the family or group."

An apport is the unexplained movement, appearance, or disappearance of an object - the mechanism for this phenomenon is unknown, but it is a commonly reported element of poltergeist cases.

Meanwhile back at the Inn...

No further incidents were reported in the first floor dressing room, so it would appear that the 'Drowned Lady' may at last have ceased to haunt it. However, paranormal events began to occur elsewhere.

- Knocking on bedroom doors, doors opening on their own, a light turning on by itself.
- A large black shape seen leaving the kitchen area around midday.
- The bell ringing in an unoccupied bar.
- A tall, dark figure going into Curtis' bedroom where a few days later one of a pair of shoes was seen to levitate for a short while.
- A hi-fi cable disappearing, only to reappear at a place already searched and in plain sight.
- A can of polish leaping from a table.
- An iPod being turned on full blast in an unoccupied bedroom.
- A bottle of brandy that had been left on the stairs disappeared, and later was found behind a TV set.

Some of this activity occurred in two rooms that had just been fully refurbished and made available for bed and breakfast. These double/twin rooms had been the scene of other minor poltergeist activity years before Tracey's family had taken over the Inn (Taylor 2006, 52).

Psychic art

Although nobody has yet been known to have photographed the ghosts at the George Inn, steps were taken to have images drawn of them. Psychic artist Dawn Lodge visited the George Inn and drew some remarkable portraits while she was there.

Dawn first became aware of having psychic power when she handled a companion's Tree Agate crystal (opaque white quartz infused with dark green branching patterns) and they watched in amazement as it took on the face of a Red Indian Chief.

Her father was keen on painting nature, but she didn't begin to develop her own artistic flair until much later in her life. "I'd always been aware of things that were going to happen" she said. "Ever since being a child, I've always known what people are thinking somehow. So that's what drew me to being a psychic artist."

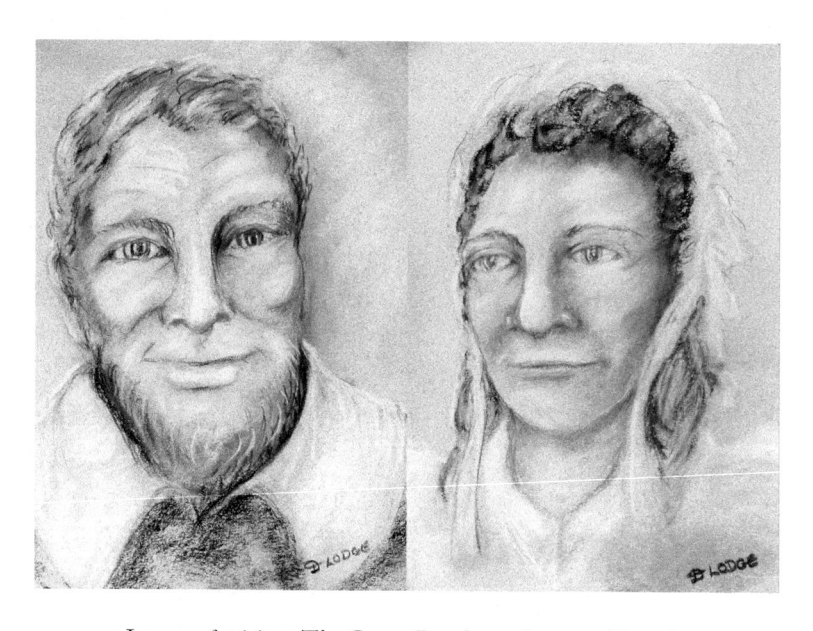

Images of spirit at The George Inn drawn by a psychic artist.

She enjoyed a pronounced talent for pareidolia - recognising random shapes as meaningful, such as in the famous Rorschach test, and smileys :) "I could see people in carpets, anything really, could just see faces and suchlike. That seems to be disappearing a little bit now, because what I'm doing more now is sensing."

It was a Tuesday night when Dawn entered the George Inn, and straight away she started to sense water. Then she began to sense that it wasn't always a pub, that it was something like a nursing home.

Upstairs, Dawn felt the atmosphere turn cold. "I knew that was to do with spirit because it was sudden. I sensed something there, and said a little request, 'stay with me, let me draw you' which I believe it did."

Whilst going down the stairs she also sensed a man with a beard. "I had a feeling they were looking after people. There was a caring feeling about the place. I sensed children. I had the feeling

Dawn working on one of her portraits.

that the lady was more in charge. She was one that did most of the caring. She was no fool, a spade was a spade. A very strong woman, but very caring.

"On her head was net-like material, and it came down in gathers at the back of the head and the straps were just hung down over her breasts. She did have long hair but she wore it up on her head. I didn't get any name from her, just 'Pentrose', referring to what, I don't know from the gentleman.

"I feel they lived here, and I think they were 'attached'. He was a jokey, laid-back gentleman - good company and he kept everybody in high spirits. He was more of a helper. I suppose with what she had to do he was more the backbone or support."

When told about the coin that rolled down the stairs, Dawn commented "I got the feeling that it was something to do with a little child.

"Also, I felt the energy of another male. He had a very round face, rustic cheeks, greying hair on the side. His hair was just strands over a balding head. His hair wasn't long, it was sort of cropped. He had rather a big nose. He wore what looked like gaiters. It was more out of the corner of my eye that I saw him because I was busy drawing (someone else). He was just sort of hovering in the woodwork, as if he was actually in the wall. I feel that he worked in the building. I don't know that he lived there. He was not like the other two."

Dowsing

In order to gain a variety of different views on the paranormal activity that was being experienced at The George, members of The Moorland Dowsers were invited to look at different pockets of activity that had been experienced within the building and the surrounding area. They were not told what had been happening before they arrived and so were coming in with fresh eyes.

Dowsing rods can be used for many things, ranging from finding water and lost objects, to archaeological surveys. They can also be used to make contact with spirits. Tony Heath, one of the dowsers with many years' experience, used the dowsing rods to get the following information: Referring initially to the male in the portrait that Dawn drew (see page 86), the dowsing rods responded to questions (the transcript has been edited for the sake of brevity).

KEY:
T   Tony (Moorland Dowsers)
C   Chris (Hidden Realms, the author)
R   Dowsing rods.

T   63 years of age. Where did he die?
R   The rods move outwards, symbolising 'Away'.
T   We have the Quaker meeting house here, which was probably something to do with him. Because to my mind that looks pretty much like an English Quaker top. He has that sort of look about him somehow of confidence and simplicity but had a belief in something. You can tell the integrity of the man. Did this man invite in visitors, Quaker visitors from the Parish, from the surrounding area?
R   Yes
T   Was this a place where they could discuss their beliefs?
R   Yes
T   There were women in this room with men together?
R   Yes
T   If the women and men were to meet separately, where would they go? Show me (he asks the rods to point in the direction).
R   The rods point to a back room.
C   Do you feel that this building had any direct attachment with the building next door at any time?
T   Yes it was part of the cottages
C   But was it as one building?
T   No, I don't see it as that. I see it as four separate cottages. The four were cottages and the fifth was the village pub.
C   Was any witchcraft or 'old magic' practiced in the area. It has been suggested in a previous investigation at The George that someone in this building in the past practised the 'old ways'.

T   I haven't had any negative thoughts at all. I haven't been stopped in my tracks. I haven't been turned back. It's all been open.
C   When I say witchcraft, I don't mean it in a negative way, it could be Wiccan or White, you know, working with nature.
T   Well of course you have to take it that the Quakers were working very much with nature. They were living within the praise of 'The Creator'. If he was here on his own he would have been seen as a target, no doubt about that and seeing people coming here from the village who were known to be trouble makers, in the church, then the priests would point a finger at them.
C   Could you ask the rods about something that has been suggested to us from spirit that occurred in the fields regarding a sudden death?
T   There seems to have been a sudden death that is connected with the present building, or even the earlier building. Was that the case? Was someone killed outside the earlier building or the present one?
R   Yes
T   Asks the rods to point in the direction that this death took place.
R   Pointed towards the part of the field where the mob had been sensed.
T   Was it anything to do with religion?
R   Yes
T   Was this a male person?
R   Yes
T   This person, was he involved with church work?
R   Yes
T   Was he someone important with the church?
R   Yes
T   Was he an Abbot?
R   No
T   But he wasn't a straight forward monk, was he someone higher?
R   Yes
T   So he had authority. What was the date this was carried out?

R   1546
C   The ecclesiastic that was murdered, which direction did he come from?
R   The rods point out towards the left which is in the area of the village called Strete.
C   Was he murdered by one person or several?
R   Seven people
T   Were these people from the village?
R   No
T   Were they local people from the surrounding area? Were they members of the local church themselves who murdered this man?
R   Yes
T   Were these just ordinary people, working class, villagers?
R   Yes
T   Did any of them actually die for their belief?
R   Yes
T   How many were imprisoned for this belief?
R   Seven
T   Were they imprisoned in something to do with the church?
R   Yes
C   Could you ask the rods if they recognise this person? (Holds up the picture of the female drawn by the psychic artist.)
R   Yes
T   Was she a local lady?
R   Yes
T   The lady died here in the bed. She is the one who is wandering. She is the spirit.
T   Did she die of natural causes?
R   Yes
T   Did she have children?
R   Yes
T   How many?
R   One

Tony, Kim and I then moved to a room at the far end of the Inn. Tony walked around the room with the dowsing rods, and described a time when it was a cottage with little furniture, and a bed up against a wall. He began speaking to the rods and found that in the year 1696 a woman aged 45 died in the bed, and her spirit still visits the room.

He asked the rods to show the path she walks, and they directed Tony back through the door and into the bar area in the middle of the pub (the area of the connecting corridor up to the darts board where Curtis has seen the lady).

Tony with the dowsing rods, mapping the layout of the older building.

We then went outside the building and used the dowsing rods to show the original building that stood where The George and the cottages now stand. The rods responded to Tony's questioning and described a tithe barn. These barns were built to store the medieval ecclesiastical tax collected from local farmers etc - one-tenth of their yield. This building was quite large and extended further into the roadway than the current Inn and cottages.

Automatic writing

During another vigil at the Inn, Hidden Realms conducted an experiment in automatic writing. It was about 3am and there had been a discussion about the drowned lady and her welfare. One of the group's sensitives wrote what may be read as 'I am not sle(e)ping' followed by a curious, almost mystical-looking glyph that resembles flames.

A further word strongly echoes the latter half of the glyph and has been interpreted as 'I happy', but it is far from clear. The writer was aware of writing something, although she didn't know what, and was not aware that she had moved her pen to another part of the paper and written the second part, 'I happy'.

Automatic writing interpreted as "Lord 1381".

Automatic writing: symbols and Churchman.

Tracey was new to this sort of thing, but Kim has a practiced hand, and wrote relatively fluently. She provided what appears to be a name and a date (unfortunately we can't be sure whether or how they relate to each other). The name, Churchman, is an unusual surname that does exist in Devon although not to my knowledge in Blackawton. However, it may not be a name but a description – a 'man of the church'.

The date, 1381, refers to a time of widespread political unrest in the countryside: for instance there was a poll tax riot in west Devon, and the famous Peasants' Revolt in southeast England. The local church (founded 1333) would have been an important focal point offering a sense of continuity amid the reverberating social chaos that followed in the wake of the Black Death. At that time in history, a church man's influence would have been considerable.

Kim also produced something that resembles a name, perhaps 'John W Ch'.

Describing how she writes, Kim said she experiences "tingling and warmness in my hand, I feel disorientated and a little dizzy. I am not completely aware of my surroundings and am completely unaware of how the pen is moving, the shapes of letters or what's being written. I do not grip the pen firmly, just let it rest in my hand, and am not aware of adjusting my grip when writing begins."

But first, she says, "I sit quietly, relax and push all thoughts from my mind. I then visualise a bubble of protective light around me. When I am happy with this I invite any spirits that are present in the room to join me (bearing in mind we only work in light). I ask if there is anything they would like to write, or draw, and explain they may use my hand to write with the pen I am holding. Sometimes spirits will talk or show me pictures before writing."

Many people try their hand at automatic writing (psychic art is perceived as requiring more training, because of the craftsmanship needed to draw faces. Although another thought on this may be that it could depend on the artistic skill of the spirit with whom you are communicating, as it is they who are allegedly guiding your hand. Kim offers a word of advice for beginners: "They need to have protection round them and say that they would like only to work with spirits in light."

The protection may be in any form you feel comfortable with, ranging from prayer to a deity, communication with a spirit guide, or even evoking a bubble of light like a 3D magic circle.

"I need the place where I am working to be quiet and a very low light or no light. Relax the mind completely and empty it of everyday thoughts. Clearing the mind can become quite easy with practise, meditation can help. Once this state is achieved, try asking if anyone present in the room would like to communicate."

Mystics often teach that heaven is here, and eternity is now, but few of us do more than glimpse that remarkable insight because our minds are too tightly focussed in a sort of tunnel vision. Psychics and clairvoyants train themselves to peer out of the rut of conventional thinking, and see what's 'out there', beyond the limits of normal consciousness.

Kim at work in The George Inn.

Exploring the paranormal is not for the faint-hearted, and having plenty of support is important, which is one reason paranormal investigation groups are so popular. It might be an exaggeration to call a good group a beacon in the gloom of the great unknown, or an oasis in the desert of man's ignorance, but then again, for many of the people that are attracted to it, that's exactly what the best groups are.

Another group nearly investigated The George Inn - the Bristol Society for Paranormal Research and Investigation - but unforeseen circumstances prevented their involvement, and instead they made arrangements to investigate Dartmouth Castle. However, the driver of the minibus took a wrong turning on the road from Totness to Dartmouth - it was the only error he made on the whole trip. He took the road to Blackawton, and drove straight past the George. Having realised his mistake he turned around and drove back the way he'd come, passing the Inn again.

It was an uncanny moment for the organisers, to discover that they had seemingly been drawn to the original target of their Devon adventure. Who would not wonder about what might have been?

Shadows of the past

A haunting that, like a recording, repeatedly replays an episode of life long ago, provides a unique window into the past. Such ghosts, like flies caught in amber, may provide a clear insight into times long past, with all the details of history standing clearly revealed before our gaze. How sad, then, that it seems so rare for us to be able to communicate with the men and women that we see.

Ghostly monks have been seen in The George Inn for at least half a century. Kathie Langford worked as a barmaid there in the 1960s and often saw a solitary figure of a hooded man, both at night and in the day. Once, she was in the lounge with the landlord and a customer, when all three of them noticed somebody walk across the room. The startled customer said "Did you see that?" And the landlord matter-of-factly pronounced they'd just seen 'Fred', as the mysterious monk was popularly called.

Kathie herself only ever witnessed the monk fleetingly, as a moving shadow seen from the corner of an eye, and sceptics are right to point out that this sort of experience may be explained as tricks of our peripheral vision. At the eye's periphery, the receptor cells are mostly rod-shaped, and only register shades of light and dark (not colour). These cells are our evolutionary adaptation for evading predators, and are especially quick to detect movement, particularly in low light.

Glimpsing a dim and featureless movement may indeed remind us of a figure enveloped in the dark folds of a monk's habit. And a local tradition of religious influence at the site, could create a compelling bias toward interpreting any vague sighting as a monk.

During one of Hidden Realms' night investigations at The George, Mike took a photograph looking down the staircase and on it there is what looks like a dark shadow at the bottom of the stairs just disappearing behind a door. Unfortunately the photograph is too dark and too undefined to include here.

All these shadowy figures though, have raised the suggestion that The George may have 'Shadow people' who, as their name suggests, are usually seen as dark shadows. There have been various reports throughout the world of such shadows being seen and then suddenly disappearing through walls, etc. Sightings of shadow people are accompanied by feelings of dread, intimidation, and fear.

Shadow people seem to be able to 'see' us and then disappear when encountered. It's thought they may exist in a different dimension to ours, and are said to resonate at a level higher than ours, which enables them to enter our dimension and prevents us following them into theirs. They have even been called time travellers, and reports appear to be increasingly frequent.

Some shadow people have been reported as wearing some type of hat. They appear to be more communicative and are a relatively new phenomenon, almost a modern perspective of a traditional ghost. The difference being that ghostly manifestations are mainly replay - re-enactments of events from the past - and do not exist in the present, so any people depicted are not aware of our presence. Shadow people are different in that they can see us and can interact with us.

But there was nothing dim or hazy about the three monks seen by landlady Tracey, they strolled along the first-floor corridor, as large as life and right in the middle of the day.

Tracey's diary

Wednesday 19th December 2007

Curtis shut the pub/private door at about 10pm at night as requested by his father as he had left it open, and as he did so a 2p coin bounced down each step missing only a few and then rolled into the pub. No one was upstairs, not even the cat.

Saturday 22nd December 2007

Zoe heard knocking on her bedroom door (spare room). She assumed it was one of us but as it was in the early hours of the morning we were all sleeping. She said that she couldn't sleep anyway and felt strange, but not scared.

Saturday 12th January 2008

Curtis awoke this morning and sat up in bed, he looked at his shoes on the floor and one of them moved up in the air and then down again whilst he was looking at it. This really freaked him out!

Sunday 13th January 2008

Bob went downstairs early to put the potatoes in the oven to roast, whilst he was in the kitchen he heard the bell in the bar ring! I was in bed and so was Curtis.

Monday 14th January 2008

Quiet during the day, but as dusk falls our friends have decided to play games this evening. Curtis cleans the pub on a Monday after school as we do not open during the day on a Monday. As he was cleaning the pub he put the polish down on the table and it flew back at him as he let go of the can. The table was not on a slant and it was not knocked in any way. This happened in the end bar at the round barrel table in the window.

In the same area, Bob was at the same time putting up all of his hi-fi stuff for this evening's quiz night. He has lost a piece of wiring which connects one part of the hi-fi to another. Without it the hi-fi is useless. He called me down to help him look for it as he was getting agitated by now. I used the torch and looked under all the units on the floor. Suddenly Bob says 'here it is!' and it is in plain view on the floor. I had just swept that area which is brightly lit anyway and it definitely wasn't there a second before. This all occurred around 5pm in the evening.

At 5.45pm, back upstairs, Bob hears music coming from the direction of Curtis's bedroom and tells Curtis, who is in the lounge at the time, to go and turn it off especially as he isn't even in his room. Curtis goes down and says that the music is coming from the end room, my old bedroom. The iPod is on and playing full blast. No one has been near that room since yesterday when I was in there stripping the wallpaper. I had been in all day and not been near the room. As it is now only 6pm I am wondering what else is in store for us this evening!

A few final tales

The Barmaid's Tale

Name: Emilie Hornblower

"It was a Monday night and we had just locked up the pub and I was talking to Tracey and Bob, the landlord and landlady. We were behind the bar. It was quite late, just after one o'clock and I saw someone walk up to the bar and when I went to serve them there was nobody there! Then I remembered the pub was locked up and so no one could have come in. I think it was a man and I felt quite shaken-up and had to go outside for some fresh air."

The Cook's Tale

Name: Sue Stevens

"One Wednesday dinnertime whilst I was in the kitchen, I noticed through the corner of my eye a shadow come through the door leading into the prep-room next to the kitchen. I thought it was my boss, Tracey. I even started talking to her, then I realised she wasn't there. No one was there.

"One Sunday night I was working by myself in the kitchen and I was cleaning down all the work surfaces. I placed a wet piece of blue kitchen roll on top of a nearby cupboard and then went over to the other side of the kitchen to take some chips out of the fryer. As I glanced round I saw the piece of kitchen roll move off the top of the cupboard work-surface, where it had been placed, and slowly come out at a right angle in mid-air and then drop to the floor. For a few seconds I felt very cold, but it quickly passed.

"It had been a wet and windy night and so there were no open windows from which a draught might have blown through and moved the towel off the worktop. Also the paper towel was wet and had been crumpled up making it quite heavy and because it was wet it could not just glide off the worktop in that manner."

The Kitchen Assistant's Tale

Name: Undisclosed

"I was heading to the kitchen to start my shift when a number of glasses just crashed from their holdings in the bar. There was nothing odd about the day it was sunny, it was an all-round nice day not the kind of day you would think of anything amiss or ghostly, it was the kind of day you would be thinking of heading to the beach.

"I'd walked in the back door to get to the kitchen and about three feet to my left four glasses literally just flung themselves to the floor from their shelves, not all from the same shelf but different ones (they each had a little wooden bar to stop the glasses from just falling out).

"I felt that was odd but I got the brush and cleaned up the mess, and later spoke to the chef. She also does the housekeeping for the rooms above and she then told me of the ghosts that wreak all kinds of hassle for the staff and had been doing so since part of the pub was turned into two houses. The pub itself was once had a huge upstairs area where the old village council would meet in pre-village hall days, and some believe that the ghosts of the pub are protesting about some of these changes."

Conclusion

The George Inn has a very interesting history and would seem to be a portal to many strange paranormal sightings. From ghostly monks, apports, dark shadows, and a ghostly 'floating' young woman, to baying mobs, murders, and poltergeists.

Key dates in its history range back to 1381, as shown with the automatic writing experiment, and include 1546 when the monk was attacked in the field behind the Inn by a group of murderous individuals, 1696 when the Quakers, as drawn by the psychic artist, inhabited the Inn, and 1747 when a mob attacked George Baker (or Barker) who was trying to defend his love Abigail.

Different methods have been used to connect with these anomalies. Psychic art, psychometry, mediumship, dowsing and scientific equipment have all played their part in unravelling the mystery that is The George. The two alleged murders that may have taken place on the field at the back of the George are approximately 200 years apart and no record can be found regarding them. But it is interesting that two different methods of investigation sensed the same type of event there.

It would appear that the building has been an important part of the village for many years, almost like the equivalent of the modern village hall. From the tithe barn that originally stood there, to the Quaker's meeting room, and also its close proximity to the church. It is possible that The George Inn still hides many ghostly secrets which hopefully will all come to light as time goes on.

Bibliography and sources

ABMC (American Battle Monuments Commission), *James W. Stephenson*, United States Government, https://www.abmc.gov/node/405801 (accessed 16 Oct 2018).

Anon 1872, Woman in White, *Dartmouth & South Hams Chronicle*, 09 August, p 3, c 2; in The British Newspaper Archive 2018, *The Dartmouth Chronicle*, Findmypast Newspaper Archive Limited, https://www.britishnewspaperarchive.co.uk/viewer/bl/0001655/18720809/030/0003 (accessed 29 Jan 2018).

Anon 1908, Ghost Hunting at Dartmouth, *Dartmouth & South Hams Chronicle*, 07 February, p 2, c 6; in The British Newspaper Archive 2018, *The Dartmouth Chronicle*, Findmypast Newspaper Archive Limited, https://www.britishnewspaperarchive.co.uk/viewer/bl/0001656/19080207/052/0002 (accessed 29 Jan 2018).

Anon 2006, *Do you know about this ghost?*, Dartmouth Chronicle & South Hams Gazette, 28 July.

Britton, Gayle 2008, *Location: Dartmouth Castle*, Bristol Society for Paranormal Research Investigation, http://bspri.org.uk/BSPRI/ (accessed 31 May 2008).

Hunter, Matt 2016, *Shocked holidaymaker claims she spotted a ghost in a picture of her son at a church*, Mail Online, https://www.dailymail.co.uk/news/article-3749316/Shocked-holidaymaker-claims-spotted-ghost.html (accessed 09 Mar 2019).

Jan Murphy is on facebook.com, search there for: Jan Murphy - Mysteries and the Paranormal.

St George 1872, The Phantom Ship of Warfleet Bay, *Dartmouth & South Hams Chronicle*, 29 March, p 2, c 1; in The British Newspaper Archive 2018, *The Dartmouth Chronicle*, Findmypast Newspaper Archive Limited, https://www.britishnewspaperarchive.co.uk/viewer/bl/0001655/18720329/032/0002 (accessed 29 Jan 2018).

Taylor, Ken 2006, *Dartmouth Ghosts & Mysteries*, Richard Webb Publisher, Dartmouth.

Townsend, Mark 2004, *Did Allies kill GIs in D-Day training horror?*, Guardian News and Media Limited, https://www.theguardian.com/uk/2004/may/16/military.usa (accessed 16 Oct 2018).

Two Jays 2019, *Ellen Whittall*, Two Jays, http://www.twojays.info/ellen-whittall (accessed 09 Mar 2019).

Picture Credits

All illustrations in the text, except those identified below, are by Christine Donnelly:

Curtis Clark 77, 79.
Dawn Lodge 40, 41, 86, back cover portraits.
Dennis Hemmings 92.
Ken Taylor 20, 51.
Lynne Maurer 29, 33.
The British Library Board (all rights reserved) 6.

Index

Agincourt House 73
alcove 15-19, 65-6
Alma Place 65-6
Ambulance HQ 62-4
Andrews, Archie 42
Anzac Street 74
apparition 74
apport 27, 84
Archway Drive 61
audio recorder 79, 81
automatic writing 93-5, 101

Baker/Barker, George 80
Bayards Cove Inn 73
Benney, Ann 84
Berry Pomeroy 45
Birchall, Wendy 37
Blackawton 69-70, 72, 73, 76-101
Blackdown Rings 69
Blackpool Sands 69
Bowsman, Sergeant 55
Bristol Society for

Paranormal Research and Investigation 50-1, 96
Britannia Royal Naval College 62, 71
Buddy 33
Burnett, Mary 59
Butterwalk 9

calendar house 29
Campbell, Mandy 21
child ghost, female 12-4, 16, 59, 69-70
child ghost, male 31, 77
children, ghosts of 73
Clark, Tracey 76-9, 81, 83, 85, 93, 97-100
Clarke, Bob 77, 81, 98-9
Clarke, Curtis 77, 79, 81, 83, 85, 92, 98-9
Clarke, John 59
classic haunting 17
Coastguard Cottages 59-60
College Way 62

Cornu 69-70
corporeal apparition 19

Dartmouth Castle 37, 39, 50-7, 96
Dartmouth Hospital 74
Dartmouth Museum 8-10, 24
Dartmouth Pottery 36
Davies, Nicholas 62
Dimes, Ursula 10
dog 81
dolls/doll's house 9-10, 31
dowsing 78, 88-92
Drimusch, Tamas & Szabo 74
Drury, Colin 67
Drury, David 35, 64
Dryden, John 55
Duke Street 9

Exercise Tiger 12, 40-47
exorcism 30

feather, white 38
fireplace 8-9, 51-2, 54-5, 57
footsteps 9, 22-3, 32, 35, 63-4, 74, 77

Gara, The 69
George Inn, The 72, 76-101
Gozdek, Rinaldo 48
Grahame, Roger 55
gravestone 75
Grove, The 72

Harbidge, Mike 78
Hauley Road 26
Hazelwood, Will 39, 74
Heath, Tony 88-92
Hemmings, Betty 40-3, 45
Hemmings, Dennis 40-3, 45
Hidden Realms Paranormal Team 40, 44, 47, 78-84, 93-5, 97
Hornblower, Emilie 99
hypnagogic hallucination 14

incorporeal apparition 19
incubus 14

Jenkins, Thelma 73
Jung, Carl 43

Keep, The 72
King James I 55
King's Room 8
Kingsbridge Cookworthy Museum 20
Kingswear 9, 28, 65-6

Langford, Kathie 96
light, turned on/off 31, 34, 61, 85
light, nature of 52-3
Lodge, Dawn 40-1, 86-9

Lower Street 73

Mann Sands 30
Market Street 21-3
Maurer, Lynne 28, 30-2
Moorland Dowsers 88-92
monk 72, 79-80, 90, 96-7, 101
Mosse, Kate 44
Mount Boone 49, 72
Murphy, Jan 9

New House Effect 23
Nethway House 9, 28-34

Old Hag, The 14, 25
Oldstone Mansion 10, 73
orb 17, 31, 34

Parry, Dan 44
peripheral vision 27, 75, 88, 96-7, 100
poltergeist 38, 61, 67-8, 83, 85, 98-100
psychic art 40, 85-8, 91, 94, 101
psychometry 83-4

remote viewing 43
replay haunting/residual energy 9, 16-7, 72
Roope, Elizabeth & Edward, 37-8
Royal Castle Hotel 67-8
Royal Coat of Arms

Sansom, John 59-60
Slapton Sands 11, 40-7
shadow people 97
sleep, lack of 15, 23
sleep paralysis 14, 25
Small, Ken 12, 46
Spinning Wheel Café 26-7
spirit, female 16, 24, 31-2, 71, 77, 81-2

spirit, male 9, 58, 68, 79-80, 88-9, 91, 99
St John Ambulance 62-4
St Michael (Blackawton) 69
St Michael (Strete) 75
St Petrox 37-9, 55
St Saviour 22-3, 48, 74
Start Bay 40
Start Bay Inn 11-20
Stenner, Rev W 75
Stephenson, James W 42
Stephenson, Stevie 41, 47
Stevens, Sue 100
Stockton, Daphne 68
Stockwell, Tony 84
Stone Tape Theory 17
Strete 75, 91
Strete Gate 58, 69
succubus 14
synchronicity 23, 43-7

Taylor, Ken 5, 50, 59, 61, 65, 71
tobacco smoke 10
Torbay Investigators of the Paranormal 50-51
Torcross 11
trigger object 51-2, 57

Vandenburg, Denice 84
Vicarage Road 69

Warfleet Bay 6
Warfleet Cottage 35-6
Watch House 59
water garden 31, 34
water theory 34
Watts, Peter & May 65
Westlake, Anne & Richard 31
Whittall, Ellen 71
witch/witchcraft 14, 25, 69-70, 89-90

Yates, Dawn & Michael 61